THE DOLLS' HOUSE
1/24 SCALE

A COMPLETE INTRODUCTION

THE DOLLS' HOUSE
1/24 SCALE
A COMPLETE INTRODUCTION

Jean Nisbett

Principal photography by Alec Nisbett

GUILD OF MASTER CRAFTSMAN PUBLICATIONS LTD

First published 1999 by
Guild of Master Craftsman Publications Ltd,
166 High Street, Lewes,
East Sussex BN7 1XU

© Jean Nisbett 1999

Reprinted 1999

ISBN 1 86108 113 8

Line drawings by John Yates
Cover photography by Anthony Bailey

Designed by Teresa Dearlove
Typeface: Garamond
Cover design by Wheelhouse Design
Colour origination by Viscan Graphics (Singapore)
Printed in Hong Kong by H & Y Printing Ltd

Photographic acknowledgements
Photographs on the following pages were supplied courtesy of:
David Booth, p.8 and p.86; Borcraft Miniatures, p.15, p.69 and p.92; Michael Browning
(Photography by June Browning), p.32 and p.91; Wendy Chalkley (Dolls of Distinction), p.44 and p.45;
Dave Chatterton (Les Chats), p.32; David Chitson (Stillmore Homes), p.13 and p.50;
Jeremy Collins, p.24 and p.87; Glenda Cunningham, p.18 and p.23, p.56 and p.68; Jacqui Dennison
(Frontshop Miniatures), p.109; Frances H. England (England's Magic), p.19; Bryan Frost, p.50 and p.51;
Greenleaf, p.13; David Hurley, p.7 and p.58; Dave Mackenzie (photograph of shop made from plans by
Jackson's Miniatures), p.91; Peter Mattinson, p.18 and p.22; G. J. Parker (Elphin Homes), p.21 and p.24;
Pat Pinnell, p.48 and also p.45 (photograph of Tudor dolls made by Coleen and Valentine Lyons);
Chris and Joan Rouch (Toptoise Design), p.20, p.21, p.22, p.24, p.39, p.42, p.88, p.90 and p.93;
Rowen Dolls' Houses, p.38; Brian Rumble (Rudeigin Beag) p.65 and p.68;
Harry Saunders (Daydream Dwellings), p.23, p.38 and p.66; Gary Sinfield (photograph of Tudor house
interior by Trigger Pond Doll Houses), p.52; Richard Stacey, p.49, p.84 and p.110;
Tetbury Miniatures, p.8 and p.41; Penny Thomson, p.13, p.44, p.51 and p.64; Keith Thorne, p.15, p.17,
p.19, p.33, p.66, p.67 and p.68; Trigger Pond Dolls' Houses p.49;
Trevor Webster, p.49; June and Albert Wells p.65 and p.70;
Paul Wells (photographs by Paul Dane), p.12, p.23, p.39, p.47 and p.83; Geoffrey Wonnacott, p.6;
World of My Own, p.54; Yesteryear Homes, p.6

Measurements
Although care has been taken to ensure that metric measurements are true and accurate, they are only
conversions from the imperial. Throughout the book instances may be found where an imperial
measurement has slightly varying metric equivalents, usually within 0.5mm either way, because in each
particular case the closest metric equivalent has been given. Care should be taken to use either
imperial or metric measurements consistently. (See also Metric Conversion Table, page 122.)

*For
Caroline,
Sarah and Guy*

Contents

Part Three *Garden and seaside style*

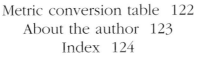

Acknowledgements

I would like to thank Elizabeth Inman for her initial advice and Stephanie Horner for carrying the project through; my editor, Cath Laing for her efficient and enthusiastic contribution; designer Teresa Dearlove for the attractive format, and my husband, Alec, for his splendid photography.

Special thanks are due to Bryan Frost, Chris Sheppard and Keith Thorne, who all made unusual buildings for me with such enthusiasm, Lesley Burgess for providing miniature food at short notice in between trips to and from America, and to Isabella Gallaon-Aoki for her help with information on the dolls' house hobby in Japan.

I am grateful to all the miniaturists whose work is featured in this book, for without their skill and patience the 1/24 hobby would simply not exist. Many of them kindly provided photographs of their work, and I would also like to thank Matthew Damper, Tony Knott, Caroline Nevill, Colin and Yvonne Roberson, Roy Stedding and Pat Venning, for loaning miniatures for our photography.

Introduction

Making a home is a basic human instinct. In real life, our ideas on decorations and furnishings are kept in check by financial considerations, but most people do their best to create a comfortable and sometimes elegant home. No wonder that decorating and furnishing dolls' houses has become a popular hobby, for here we can indulge our tastes and ambitions to the full.

This dolls' house typifies Georgian style with a 'stone' facade, a six-panelled front door, plain door case and a symmetrical arrangement of sash windows.

The modern interest in dolls' houses began in the United States and spread rapidly to Britain, France and the Netherlands; it is now a growing hobby in Australia, New Zealand and Japan.

This tiny house would appeal to children and adult hobbyists alike.

In the eighteenth century, dolls' houses were owned by a privileged few wealthy and aristocratic ladies. There was no need for a standard size and, as there was plenty of space for display, 1/10 scale was often chosen. In Victorian times, the height of rooms and the size of furniture was sometimes disproportionate. In the modern dolls' house hobby, 1/12, in which 1 inch represents 1 foot, soon became accepted as the international standard for craftspeople making houses, miniature furniture and accessories.

More recently, 1/24 scale – a big enough jump to be distinctively different – has been adopted with enthusiasm by many makers and hobbyists. It is equally appealing in that such tiny representations have their own fascination and charm. And it is the reason for this book, as decorating and furnishing a house in this small size needs a different approach from that of the larger 1/12 scale. For craftspeople, it creates new problems, in terms of design and execution, for which solutions need to be found; for the hobbyist, it represents a completely different challenge.

My first 1/24 house was very tiny – a 'mouse house' intended for a young child – but one which became so popular with adult hobbyists that the maker is still producing the same model many years later. When I decorated and furnished that house, there were very few miniaturists making in such a small size. I was lucky to find a craftsman who was keen to extend his skills, or my little house might have remained unfurnished.

I made my own accessories and bought additional furnishings as interest in the new scale increased and more items became readily available. I also discovered early on that it is possible to include a few 1/12 pieces, provided that they are carefully chosen (see page 97). I enjoyed decorating and furnishing this charming little house, which has now been handed over to my youngest granddaughter for her to enjoy in her turn.

This book aims to give you all the information you need to know about 1/24 scale, whether you are a complete beginner or already enjoying the dolls' house hobby. Part One tells you what is available and where to find it, lists paints and materials and tells you where to get them and gives basic information on the techniques used for decorating, which is then expanded in detail in Part Two. There is also advice on making up kits. The cost of both furniture and houses is discussed, so that you will be aware of both inexpensive and more lavish options, to help you to choose what suits you best.

Part Two gives detailed practical advice, illustrated by the decoration and completion of my latest 1/24 scale houses, small buildings and a series of room box settings and gardens. The work of many miniaturists is pictured throughout this book, and I hope that this will provide inspiration to those who have not yet tried the smaller scale. A list of makers is also included (see page 120).

Everyone can appreciate the abundance of suggestions for working in this small scale, and for those already familiar with 1/24, I hope that there will be something new to give further encouragement and interest in this engrossing hobby.

Part One •
Planning

A Dutch bureau cabinet in walnut with marquetry inlays (in 1/24 scale) displayed on a 1/12 scale side table. The cabinet has working locks and eight secret drawers. The detail is astonishing and shows just what can be achieved by a master craftsman.

1 *The Scale*

My reaction when I first saw a 1/24 dolls' house was one of delight, followed by amazement at the small size of the rooms – but then a moment of doubt. How could anyone with average-size hands manage to decorate and arrange furniture in spaces that were rarely more than 7in (178mm) wide by 6½in (165mm) deep, and around 6in (152mm) high? Naturally I wanted to see if I could achieve this and was soon hard at work.

Two almost identical Tudor houses demonstrating the advantage of 1/24 scale to the hobbyist with limited space for display.

To anyone who shares my initial feelings of astonishment, or even disbelief, I can offer reassurance. After only a few hours thinking out revised approaches to interior design, and then actually tackling these smaller decorative schemes, the reduced scale seemed perfectly normal. When I then went back to look at one of my 1/12 dolls' houses, it seemed huge. It is only a matter of adjustment, which you will find is quickly made.

The 1/24 scale has been part of the dolls' house hobby for many years in the United States. When it began to appear in Britain, a gradually increasing number of professional miniaturists relished the challenge of producing even smaller work. Initially, one or two items of furniture were displayed on stands at miniatures fairs, at first attracting more admiration than purchases, but soon orders were placed and the new scale became a fully accepted part of the hobby. There are now more than one hundred British minia-turists making at least part of their output in 1/24, with some, especially dolls' house makers, for whom it has become a major specialization.

A 1/24 chess table made in ebony and rosewood. The board measures 1⅛ x 1⅛in (18 x 18mm). The chess pieces, turned and carved in ebony and boxwood, are set in wax so that they can be rearranged to show a game in progress.

Scale comparisons

The 1/24 scale is not always fully understood; in fact, at one time it was termed 'half-scale', which added to the confusion. What was unclear from this was that the measurements of a piece of miniature furniture need to be halved in all directions to give only ⅛ of the volume – or overall size – of a similar piece in 1/12.

It may be useful to show some pictures of similar miniatures in each scale, side-by-side, for comparison and to help you to adjust to 1/24.

These elaborately carved oak chests are both based on the same Tudor original. Such minute detail is the work of a master miniaturist.

Four-poster beds again show the size differential between the two scales. The 1/12 bed hangings are based on those on William Morris's bed at Kelmscott. Astonishingly, the 1/24 hangings are of hand-knitted lace.

Chests of drawers in either scale are a test of a miniaturist's skill. The 1/24 version is made from fine-grained mahogany while the 1/12 is made from yew. Both bowls are porcelain, which a skilled maker can produce in 1/24.

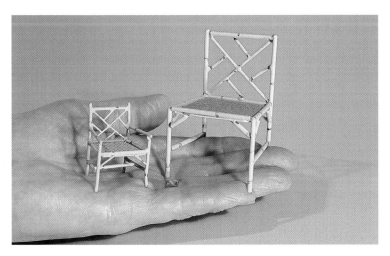

Both 'bamboo' chairs are made in metal and based on a miniature in the sitting room in Queen Mary's dolls' house at Windsor Castle. The specialist metalworker can work as accurately to 1/24 as to 1/12.

Chippendale produced many variations of the interlacing on the pierced central splat of his chairs, and the miniaturist's skill is tested to the full with this complicated arrangement, shown in both 1/24 and in 1/12.

Victorian-style prie-dieu chairs were designed for kneeling, not sitting, and were used for prayer. These examples are made in mahogany and upholstered in the same way as for full-size furniture.

While looking at the close-up pictures, you will be able to see the miniatures in a way that would be impossible without using a magnifying glass. Some remarkable work is produced by leading miniaturists who enjoy the challenge of making a piece as meticulously in 1/24 as in 1/12, but carving, for example, can be so small that the fine detail is almost invisible to the naked eye. The camera clearly shows not only the beauty of the piece, but also the detail, the grain of the wood or the size of a stitch, magnified many times.

The dedicated craftsperson aims to achieve perfection in every detail. For the hobbyist, who will not be looking through a magnifying glass or a camera lens most of the time, such a high standard is not necessary, and working in 1/24 will be no more exacting than working in 1/12.

Examples of 1/24 measurements

In countries where metric measures are used and a one-foot ruler is not available, 1/25 scale may be preferred. In this, 4cm (1⅝in) represents 1m (39½in). For all practical purposes, 1/24 and 1/25 are the same, as the difference cannot be distinguished by eye.

Measurements are approximate, because individual items will vary.
If in doubt, measure up objects in your own home and scale them down.

Rooms (typical size)	Depth	6½–7in (165–178mm)
	Ceiling height	5–6in (127–152mm)
	Width	6½–7in (165–178mm)
Furniture		
Four-poster bed	Length	3½in (89mm)
	Height	3⅜in (86mm)
	Width	2½–3in (64mm)
Single bed	Length	3¼in (82mm)
	Width (3ft bed)	1½in (38mm)
Dining chair	Height to seat	¾in (19mm)
	Height of back varies	
Armchair/Sofa	Height to seat	⅝in (16mm)
	Height of back and length vary	
Dining table	Height	1¼in (32mm)
	Length and width vary	
	Diameter of circular table	2–3in (51–76mm)
Dolls		
Gentleman	Height	3in (76mm)
Lady		2¾in (70mm)
Toddler		1⅛in (30mm)
Baby		¾in (19mm)

The advantages and disadvantages of 1/24

One major bonus for most of us is that 1/24 dolls' houses are, in general, less expensive than 1/12. Working in small scale is economical, because there are many low-cost materials which can be utilized for decoration (see pages 29–31).

Another advantage is the lack of weight. You can pop your entire 1/24 house or room box into a holdall or shopping bag and take it to a dolls' house club meeting to share with your friends.

There are some disadvantages, too, but all potential problems have their solutions and I hope that I have checked out most of them. Here are a few things which may occur to you if you are starting on your first small-scale project.

Q Will it be difficult to reach into rooms with such low ceiling heights when decorating or arranging furniture?

A Most makers are aware of this and are ingenious in incorporating a number of openings and removable fittings.

The mill house is complete with a balcony and a mill wheel which turns; both can be removed for decoration. The maker has taken trouble with the details and not forgotten the needs of the interior decorator; stairs, balustrade and gallery all lift out easily.

Q I have never tackled carpentry. Will I need to put in fiddly wooden fixtures and fittings?
A Fixtures and fittings can be simplified; in tiny rooms too much detail will not show to advantage. Thin stripwood, which can be cut with scissors, can be used to make, for example, a fireplace.

Q Where can I find ornaments and accessories which are small enough?
A Accessories in 1/24 scale are available at miniatures fairs and by mail order. Many items too small to be made in wood are cast in metal, ready to be painted. Items in 1/12 scale are often suitable. For example, the smaller sizes of cooking pans intended for 1/12 are just right on a 1/24 range. A Chinese vase can be included as a floor-standing ornament in a 1/24 room, rather than placing it on a table.

An example of a 1/12 ornament which can be used in a 1/24 room (see page 97).

Q Where can I find kits, furniture, fixtures and fittings?
A In the United States, the majority of dolls' house outlets supply fixtures and fittings in both scales. This is not yet the case in Britain, although more and more shops have some space devoted to 1/24. If you are not within easy reach of a retail stockist, the answer is mail order. Dolls' house magazines carry advertisements by both makers and suppliers, whose catalogues offer everything from dolls' house kits to the smallest miniature.

A set of shelves to hang on a wall is supplied assembled, ready for staining or polishing. The saucers are made of pewter which can be painted.

Many of these suppliers also exhibit at miniatures fairs, details of which are advertised in dolls' house magazines and elsewhere, so you will be able to look before you buy. Makers will sometimes make to order something which is not in their standard range – it is always worth asking if you have a special request.

Improvization

The dolls' house hobby gives plenty of scope for lateral thinking. Finding new uses for leftovers is both economical and rewarding.
- Spare 1/12 picture-frame mouldings can be used as cornice (see page 75).
- Sections of wallpaper borders make good friezes.
- Scraps of velvet or suede can be used as carpets (see page 98).
- Textured art papers simulate plastered walls (this is much less messy than doing the plastering yourself), and marbled card makes beautiful floors (see pages 29 and 31).
- A short length of wooden moulding will make a shelf.
- A plastic bottle top can be transformed into a table when painted, or it can even become a pottery kiln (see page 61).

Sharing your ideas with friends is rewarding. Dolls' house clubs are popular; the interchange of ideas and methods stimulates many new uses for bits and pieces. Again, see advertisements in dolls' house magazines to find your local club.

Shopping list

The craft shop

Try using modelling materials to make floors and food, and search for tiny beads to use as vases. Jewellery 'bits and pieces' can also be transformed into vases and light fittings (see page 79 and page 97).

The railway modeller shop

Railway modelling materials are essential for gardens. Buy inexpensive stripwood to make plain skirting boards, door frames and shelves, and ask for a shade card showing the range of model enamels and varnishes.

The stationer

Check out the range of adhesives and choose the correct type to suit the material you plan to use. Stock up on Blu-tack, Gripwax and similar products.

Specialist paper suppliers

Look for unusual textured papers and cards for decorating walls and floors.

Card and gift shop

Postcards can be useful to adapt for trompe l'oeil effects and wall coverings (see page 79 and page 98).

Art suppliers

Foamboard is ideal for making the bases and liners of room boxes (see page 93). Note that art shop masking tape is available in a choice of widths and is more suitable for miniaturists than decorator's masking tape. It is also cheaper.

2 Choosing your house

Even if you are new to the hobby, you will probably have an idea of what kind of dolls' house you want. Town or country, formal or informal, period or modern – there is plenty of choice.

Many hobbyists begin on 1/24 after they have completed one or more larger scale dolls' houses, so this can be a time for imaginative schemes and unusual rooms. If you cannot fit in all your choices, it will be more rewarding

Prentice Cottage is a copy of a cottage in Suffolk, and was commissioned by the Puppenhaus Yoshima Museum in Japan as an example of a typical small English home. The black-and-white colour scheme makes a delightful contrast with the red roof tiles, which were individually cut, fitted and painted by the maker. Good access is provided to all the rooms by side and roof openings.

A medieval house with a later, Jacobean extension. Interior decoration and furnishing might reflect the lapse of time between the date of the original aisled hall and the later timber-framed addition. The dolls' house is made from papier-mâché as infill for the timber framing, by the artist maker, who enjoys working with this unusual technique. She uses her painting skills to reproduce the colours of worn stone.

to concentrate on the themes you really want and imagine non-essentials out of sight.

Beginners, on the other hand, will probably prefer to include standard room arrangements. In a two-room house, the kitchen and living room can be combined, as is now common in real life, leaving enough space for a bedroom. A 1/24 house or room box should be less expensive than one in 1/12, so over time, you may be able to invest in a second miniature home to try out other schemes and period styles. For future use, keep a note of your better ideas which will not fit in this time around.

Here are some examples to consider; you may find something which will link up with your initial ideas or even set you off in a new direction. Visit some miniatures fairs and dolls' house shops before you buy, and send for makers' illustrated catalogues to look through (see the advertisements in specialist dolls' house magazines).

Assembling a house from a kit

This option will appeal to many hobbyists. Most kit houses in 1/24 scale are American, and are available through British stockists as well as in the United States. Assembly requires no carpentry skills and is usually achieved by means of slot-together sections.

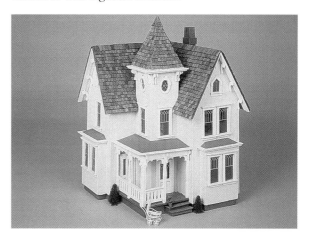

Above **The Fairfield is an American version of a Victorian-style dolls' house; it has six rooms plus a porch with pretty detailing and is accessible from all sides. Four fireplaces and roof shingles are included with the kit. The completed house measures 15in (381mm) wide, 16in (406mm) deep and 20in (508mm) high.**

Below **This cottage ornée is a limited edition kit, which is also available completed and decorated. It is based on Vine Cottage, designed by John Nash for Blaise Hamlet, near Bristol, a unique village built 1810–11, where each cottage is in a slightly different style. Further limited edition kits are planned, based on some of the other cottages which Nash designed.**

If you have assembled a dolls' house kit before, you will have a good idea of how long it may take to complete the project. American kits are fanciful creations and are likely to have plenty of interest in the form of porches, balconies and intriguingly shaped roofs with turrets. The basic structure will be of thin wood, as it is intended to be covered with surface decoration; siding and shingles may be provided with the kit, or available as optional extras.

Most British dolls' house makers prefer to provide an assembled wooden house ready for decoration, but there are exceptions. Plans are also available from some British makers. Assembly will be more challenging than an American kit, but should be within the capabilities of anyone who enjoys woodwork, and detailed instructions are provided.

Hints on making up a kit house

- Check first that all the parts are included in the kit. Lay them out and familiarize yourself with them.
- Read the instructions provided, check the parts mentioned at each stage of the assembly and make sure that you under-stand how they fit together.
- Sand each piece with fine glasspaper, grade 000.
- Check that any pre-cut slots or grooves are the right size to take slot-in parts. You may need to make minute adjustments by sanding to ensure a perfect fit.
- Assemble each stage 'dry' and check that all is correct before you use wood glue. Once the glue has set it will be impossible to undo.
- While the glue is setting, it is best to hold the pieces firmly together with masking tape, because it will take several hours until full strength is achieved.
- Ensure that the walls and floors are at right angles, or you could end up with a leaning house. Check the angles with a set square. It is advisable to make a jig to support the structure while the glue dries. If you do not have an appropriately equipped workshop, make a jig by using blocks of wood with

perfectly squared corners, or improvise by using piles of books.
- It can be useful to paint structures and other internal features before fixing them in place. Check whether some of the room decoration might be done more easily before assembly.
- Allow plenty of time. It will take longer than you anticipate.

A kit house

A kit house has other advantages apart from being economical. Decoration will be easier because it is possible to paint window frames and small trims before they are fixed in place permanently. In addition, a real feeling of satisfaction can be gained from assembling your own dolls' house.

A ready-made house

The cheapest ready-made house will be a basic, unpainted 'shell', leaving you to decorate inside and out. Most such houses are architecturally accurate versions of period houses, made of strong plywood, or MDF (medium density fibreboard), which will look equally good with a simple painted finish or with realistic cladding added. Internal features such as chimney breasts and fireplaces may be provided.

This mill house is country style with an extra touch of imagination. It has half-timbered walls, a neatly chamfered chimney and two opening doors. It is supplied undecorated.

Other options

Not everyone wants to undertake the entire decoration themselves, and more expensive houses may be offered with the exterior finished, leaving you to concentrate on the inside. This type of house is a good choice if you want, for example, a thatched cottage, or a town house with elaborate architectural detail, which you might prefer the maker to provide.

The realistic thatch, herringbone brickwork, timbers and leaded windows on this cottage home are a credit to the maker's skill and patience. The bricks are made of wood and then painted.

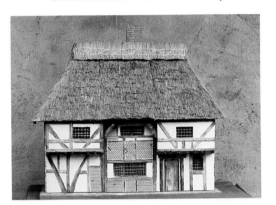

More expensively, you can order a house from a craftsman who will provide everything you specify. You will be able to ask for the type of finish you want, and decide exactly how much decoration will be included. Such a house will be an heirloom to pass on to your family and will give unending pleasure. The price may be considerable, but it should be a good investment.

Room boxes and vignettes

The 1/24 hobby is not only about complete dolls' houses. It is also concerned with single-room settings, arranged in open-fronted room boxes. These individual scenes are delightful projects to tackle and allow the hobbyist more freedom to explore different styles and periods than a whole dolls' house, where everything needs to be in keeping. A series of room sets take up very little space.

A realistic scene arranged in a room box assembled from a kit. The furniture, by the same maker, is available separately either with distressed paint finish or plain. Accessories, dolls and food can be added to personalize the scene.

A vignette

A vignette, which can be hung on the wall, is another space saver. The box should be only 2–3in (51–76mm) deep, the front surrounded by a picture frame. There is enough depth for a scene which will give the illusion of a three-dimensional room yet take up no more wall surface than a small picture (see page 104).

Room boxes are practical, because they can be moved easily if your only work surface is a table which will be needed for other purposes during the day. They can be a complete project or a try out for decorating and furnishing a dolls' house. With a room box, you can experiment to see whether a particular style really appeals to you.

If, like me, you are fascinated by modern architecture and design, which is way ahead of current styles in ready-made dolls' houses, room boxes offer an opportunity to complete an unusual room and incorporate features which appeal to you most from the pick of modern styles. Exhibitions and articles in magazines can spark off many ideas for such projects.

Individual period and modern rooms are pictured and discussed in detail in Part Two, with ideas on alternative schemes and things to make for inclusion.

Wooden room boxes can be purchased with a glass or Perspex sliding or lift-out front to ensure that the contents are free from dust, and are available ready made or as a kit. A box made from foamboard is rigid and reasonably strong and you can make your own open-fronted box very easily (see page 93).

A stylish modern figure which could be included in a variety of settings. It looks magnificent as a large work in a 1/24 hallway (see page 103), but could equally be used as a desktop figure in 1/12. The sculpture was hand-modelled and then cast in bronze resin by the maker.

3 *Deciding on a style*

Once you have decided whether to assemble a kit or buy one ready made, you can choose an architectural style. Unless you plan an updated, modern interior, your decorative schemes, patterns and furnishings will all follow through from the period of the house itself.

A genuine English Tudor house is unique, evoking the atmosphere of past times through dark, oak-filled rooms with many paned leaded windows, beamed ceilings and the patina of age. An eighteenth-century house in New England holds enchantment too, with elegant rooms containing furniture which is subtly different from the English equivalent.

Above **An American Colonial-style house with interesting windows, veranda and porch. The elaborate fretwork roof ridging is hand-carved and gilded.**

A French peasant farmhouse is a joy to miniaturize if you like distressing paintwork, whereas the English or American farm will be more likely to be portrayed as well cared for. For modern ideas, you need look no further than the houses in the nearest town or city, or failing that, the pages of home decoration magazines, which, to me at least, are a never failing source of inspiration.

Here is a brief list of possibilities; style variations are illustrated and described in detail in Part Two, with ideas on suitable colour schemes, decorative materials and furnishings, some of which you can make yourself.

Period styles

Tudor

A splendid dolls' house version of a Tudor house with medieval origins, complete with carving copied from existing examples. This innovative dolls' house is cast in resin, making it more affordable than the hand-carved wooden prototype. This method makes it possible for the maker to repeat the same design in a shorter time.

There are many variations on Tudor style, from a house with medieval origins to a tall town mansion. The exterior of a Tudor house can be more tricky to decorate than a plain, classical facade, but is well worth the effort (see pages 49–51). Tudor houses have existed for over four hundred years, and many real houses are still lived in very comfortably today with the interiors sensitively updated to retain period features, but with the added benefits of modern plumbing and central heating. The hobbyist can also have the best of both worlds with a Tudor dolls' house and an updated interior (see page 60).

The English cottage

The English cottage is first choice for many hobbyists, especially those who would really like to own and live in the real thing. The miniature cottage is always pretty, and most dolls' cottage exteriors are fully finished by the maker, so that only interior decoration is necessary. In reality, such buildings are undoubtedly picturesque, but originally they were cramped and often also damp. The dolls' house version will be enchanting, if somewhat romanticized by the omission of these flaws.

This beautifully decorated English cottage was made by an American miniaturist who has studied cottage styles during many visits to England.

The seaside cottage

Cottages are not confined to the depths of the country. Attractively painted, simple cottages, originally dwellings for fishermen, have now become holiday homes in many seaside towns. For the miniaturist, a 1/24 cottage of this type can be great fun to decorate and furnish, with fishy items included to show its original purpose, or even updated to modern use. A twentieth-century beach chalet or beach hut is the ideal smaller seaside project, complete with whiffs of nostalgia for childhood holidays (see page 117).

Georgian

Georgian style is a perennial favourite and in 1/24 it is possible to have a complete mansion which takes up very little space. A house similar to the one illustrated will be a long-term project, as there is as much to keep a hobbyist occupied as when dealing with a 1/12 house of grand proportions.

Victorian

Victorian houses have plenty of detail on the facade, and the rooms can be filled to overflowing with miniatures, as ornament and decoration is the essence of this style. A Victorian house is a good choice for someone who wants to create a lived-in look. The kitchen, in particular, is the favourite room for many (see page 89).

Left **A linked pair of fishermen's cottages – they are not identical, as one has an extension at the side. Decorating the interiors in contrasting styles would make an interesting project.**

Below **An accurate Victorian facade which conceals an unusual interior. It was commissioned as a cabinet in which to keep private papers, and four rooms inside are designed to be used as storage space.**

Twentieth-century style

Mackintosh

Charles Rennie Mackintosh has had a continuing influence on modern design, and his colour schemes and furniture are currently enjoying a revival. He was the first truly modern architect and designer, the forerunner of Bauhaus style and Art Deco, both of which followed his lead in using white with strong colour accents (see page 94). His distinctive style is equally impressive when miniaturized and has become popular with hobbyists who relish the challenge of modern design.

Above **The simplicity and originality of Mackintosh's Janitor's House for Scotland Street School in Glasgow has been copied faithfully in this 1/24 dolls' house version.**

Single rooms are preferred by Japanese hobbyists rather than a complete dolls' house. Lack of clutter and a calm atmosphere are valued, and in this miniature every detail has been considered carefully.

The Japanese influence

Mackintosh was influenced by traditional Japanese style, and his cool, sparsely furnished interiors were in deliberate contrast to the overfilled rooms in vogue when he began his career.

A typical Edwardian suburban home, which, when built, appeared ultra-modern after the over elaboration of late Victorian style.

Edwardian

The Tudor influence

In the early years of this century, grand houses built by Sir Edwin Lutyens incorporated many elements of Tudor style. His houses fitted well into the English landscape, and inside the emphasis was on comfort.

The smaller Edwardian house, a mass-produced version of the revamped Tudor style, influenced suburban house building for years to come. Inside, the fashion for oak furniture was almost obligatory.

1920–30s

The Tudor revival continued until the outbreak of the Second World War, when house building in Britain virtually ceased. Rows of identical, suburban houses all had their gable ends and mock beams. These houses were well built and comfortable. For many people living in this type of house today, a 1/24 version would provide a delightful project. The rooms could be furnished in Art Deco or modern style.

This type of house was so popular in the 1930s that such homes still form the bulk of domestic housing in towns and cities across Britain today. Attention to detail by the dolls' house maker includes stained glass embellishments to porch windows.

Shops

A one- or two-room house with a good-sized window on the ground floor can be used as a shop and there are many purpose-built dolls' house shops available. Many miniaturists enjoy shops, because they are so versatile: they can be used as a display unit for a collection of treasured miniatures, as storage for pieces awaiting transfer to an unfinished dolls' house, or combined with living accommodation for the shopkeeper.

A shop can be multipurpose; this attractive one-room building extends outside with café seating, and there is also a postbox on the wall, offering several choices of use for the hobbyist to enjoy.

Quick-reference style guide

Doors and windows provide an instant identification to both period and modern house styles. Here is a pictorial guide from medieval to the 1930s.

Carved wooden figures stand guard each side of the medieval entrance, while gilded stone heads provide a decorative flourish to the windows. The lintel above the doorway is a riot of carving.

A heavy beam, apparently marked by the passage of time, tops this Tudor leaded window. The stonework is painted to resemble Oxfordshire stone.

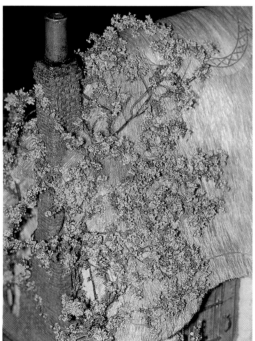

Roses round the door – everyone's idea of the typical English cottage.

The perfect Georgian entrance. This miniature version has all the detail of the original pediment and pilasters. The windows are the typical six-over-six arrangement of panes and the railings and handrail to the steps indicate that this is a town rather than a country house.

Georgian and early Victorian styles overlapped by at least twenty years, particularly in the provinces, where builders took longer to adapt to new fashions in architecture. What might seem a standard Georgian entrance on this 1/24 dolls' house is a copy of a real house built several years after Victoria became Queen, although the windows are no longer the typical eighteenth-century arrangement of panes.

White paintwork, stained glass panels in the front door and square bay windows were the hallmark of Edwardian style. Edwardians saw nothing strange about mixing features from different periods; the door is topped by a Georgian-style pediment, while the gable shows fake, rather than integral, timbers, based on an idea of Tudor style which was much admired.

The Art Deco influence shows strongly in the curved porch and oval window in the front door. The bay window is now rounded rather than square. The front gate, too, has an Art Deco motif.

4 *Decoration*

finished schemes in two complete houses and a series of smaller buildings, individual rooms and garden settings.

Pictorial references and suggestions about materials and paints should make life easy for both beginner and someone looking for new ideas. There are many variations on styles and the ones given may set you off in a new direction. It can be difficult, sometimes, to decide how best to deal with tight corners or slightly inaccessible spots in 1/24. Again, solutions are given and illustrated with pictures of my own and others' work.

The whole purpose of a hobby is that it should be pleasurable and absorbing, but not too much like hard work. It is for relaxation, not stress, a chance to unwind from everyday cares. Dolls' house decoration is like creating a stage set – if an economical and easy-to-use material or idea works and looks good, then there is no need to do something complicated. The finished effect is the important thing, not the way you achieve it.

Here is some basic guidance on decorating in 1/24 scale. There are suggestions for using card and paper to represent wall coverings and flooring, and advice on choosing paint colours to give the best effect in tiny rooms. These initial ideas are carried through in Part Two, with detailed instructions and pictures of

Another view of the Georgian house shown earlier (see page 1). The roof is designed to lift off, providing a useful storage space for small tools while decorating, and later for furniture waiting to be arranged in the rooms.

Never work when you are tired, because it is then that mistakes are most likely to occur. Wait until another day to finish off flooring or put in skirting boards.

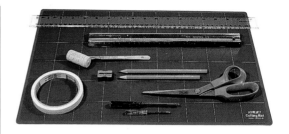

These simple tools are essential for working in 1/24.

Planning

Plan carefully – it will be well worth it, even though you may be longing to start on the actual decorations. Remember that you are not only decorating and furnishing rooms, but also creating a lifestyle. This can be wealthy or folksy, but work out a consistent theme so that it can be reflected in the living arrangements.

Whether you are tackling a complete dolls' house or an individual room setting, careful planning will make all the difference to the finished result.

Do some research

Check out the details of your chosen style and period. It can be useful to look at pictures in decoration magazines and books relating to period homes. You might want to update the interior of a period house (see page 60) or in a more modern house, include fashions for styles which recur periodically. For example, Regency was revamped in the 1920s and Tudor reproduction furniture was popular in the 1930s.

Tools

For general dolls' house decoration and fittings, the minimum of simple tools is sufficient. For 1/24 work, only the following tools are essential:
■ Cutting mat with a squared grid (from an art shop or stationers),
■ Craft knife with replaceable blades,
■ Metal ruler with a raised edge, for use as a cutting guide,
■ Sharp scissors,

■ Small screwdrivers,
■ Pencils (and a sharpener),
■ Masking tape ½in (13mm) wide.

Safety first

Treat all cutting tools with respect.

Using a craft knife
1 Always check before you cut that your free hand is behind the blade and not in front of it.
2 Never use cutting tools if you are tired, when it becomes too easy to make a mistake. There is always another day.
3 Always put a craft knife down while you check or adjust the position of the work. It is easy to forget that you are holding it and to nick yourself.
4 If the blade is not retractable, store safely by digging it into a cork.

Adhesives

A general-purpose clear adhesive is suitable to fix most internal fittings in 1/24, as there will not be any thick wooden pieces which might need something stronger.

To fix down card flooring again use a general-purpose adhesive, taking care to use sufficient around the edges to make sure that they do not lift up. Wait until the glue becomes tacky before pressing the card into place and tape it down with masking tape until the glue is set. Alternatively, attach the card with double-sided adhesive tape; stick the adhesive tape to the floor first and press the card on top.

Using paint

One of the first things that young children learn at school is to enjoy using paint. This enjoyment continues into adult hobbies, and one of the most rewarding has to be decorating dolls' houses.

The decorations will not have to stand up to everyday wear and tear – you can achieve anything from simplicity to ornate effects and gain an immense feeling of satisfaction, without aching muscles afterwards. You can also use your talent creatively to produce worn, aged-looking effects (see pages 50 and 51). It beats full-size decorating every time. Don't be afraid to experiment with colour, but try out your mixes on card before beginning on the house.

Suitable types of paint for dolls' house decoration

Decorator's paints

Modern paint manufacturers produce histori-cally accurate 'heritage' colours. These are available in inexpensive sample sizes which are ideal for the dolls' house decorator.

Textured paints

Textured paints will create the effect of a roughly plastered wall, or a garden path. Brush on one coat before colourwashing. Look out for textured stencil paints in small sizes.

Gouache

This is supplied in tubes and there is a huge range of colours available. It is an ideal paint for producing unusual, glowing colours. Mix a few drops with water-based emulsion and dilute with a little water to use as a colourwash on walls. It can be wiped off before it dries thoroughly and further colour added to give a random effect. Finish with a coat of varnish, because it is not waterproof.

Acrylic paint

This is also supplied in tubes ready to mix with water-based emulsion and is easy to use and quick drying. Mix as for gouache. To colourwash on wooden furniture, add water only. Finish with a coat of matt varnish

Varnish

Varnishes are available as clear (gloss), matt, semi-matt or coloured. Gloss is too shiny to use on 1/24 and coloured varnish should be used with caution as it is thicker than clear varnish. Matt or semi-matt finishes are the best choice on 1/24 dolls' houses.

Woodstain

Not exactly a paint, but ideal for colouring wooden Tudor beams and furniture. Wipe on with a cloth or a cotton bud. It is quick drying.

Model enamel

Useful for front doors, stair rails and balusters and metal ornaments. No undercoat is necessary and one coat will cover well and dry quickly. Gloss, matt, semi-matt and metallic finishes are available, as well as the new, seemingly magical finish Metalcote, which transforms wood or card into metal in a matter of minutes (see pages 61 and 96).

Hints on painting

■ Provided you seal tubes and cans properly after use, modern paints keep well, often for years, so that you can acquire a useful stock of different finishes to be used when you think of new ideas for decoration on furniture or accessories.

- If you are using up paint from a large can, decant some into a yoghurt pot and reseal the main can while your work. It is natural to wipe the brush on the edge of the container each time you dip it into the paint, and this can cause a sticky build up which will prevent the can closing properly.
- A painted marble effect looks good on table tops. Use model enamel or acrylic paint to add one or two colours over a base coat. Find a pictured example to copy – you will find it is really easy. The secret is to brush on the paint gently with feather-light strokes, and do not overdo it.

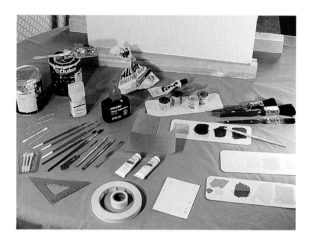

Lay out paints and brushes neatly so that they are ready to hand when needed. Shade cards for testing paint colours and for later reference can be useful.

A pretty occasional table; the base has been painted to simulate the look of antique, worn gilding, and the top is painted as marble.

Choosing paintbrushes

Size ⅜in (approximately 10mm) or ½in (approximately 13mm) decorator's paintbrushes are the most suitable for painting walls, and roofs. For smaller details you will need artist's brushes from size 0 to 5. Do not buy the top quality which are very expensive and too soft for painting wooden surfaces. The cheapest artist's brushes are ideal, firm enough for the purpose and not too costly to throw away before they become completely worn out.

There are many short stages in decorating each part of a miniature house or object, using a variety of paints, and brushes will need to be cleaned or washed many more times than with normal use. Replace as soon as necessary to achieve good results.

For a perfect finish, always begin on a new house with new paintbrushes.

Care of paintbrushes

- Never use the same paintbrush for both paint and varnish. Keep a separate brush for each purpose.
- Clean brushes immediately after use. Emulsion paint, gouache and acrylic can be washed out with water. Clean with white spirit (mineral spirits) after using undercoat, decorator's paint, model enamel or varnish and finish with a wash in water with a little liquid detergent added.

Wallpapers

With the exception of cottage and ultra-modern interiors, which in general look best simply colourwashed, most dolls' house rooms can be papered. Anything which can be pasted on to a wall is 'wallpaper', even fabric or card. American wallpapers in 1/24 are plentiful – look out for imported papers if you live in Britain. Alternatively, many low-cost papers not originally designed for use in dolls' houses will be suitable.

Examples of cards for flooring, wall covering and trompe l'oeil ideas.

Specialist paper shops and some stationers stock large sheets of both machine and handmade papers in attractive colours. As well as patterned designs, there are textured papers which will give the effect of a plastered wall, and you can colourwash over these to create a new colour scheme in each room. The cost and size of a large sheet will vary but one such sheet will in general be no more expensive than buying several smaller pieces of miniaturized wallpaper.

Giftwrap designs, so useful when working in 1/12, are often too large, although occasionally you may come across something with a border pattern which can be used by judicious cutting. Another source of wallpaper is from magazines and brochures, where there is often a colour page simply begging to be used as background (see page 114). Start a collection of anything you think may come in useful, for example small-scale pictures of wall surfaces and flooring. Before you throw away junk mail brochures, it is worth looking through them to see whether there is anything you can use. Salvaged materials are free and will help you to create original schemes.

Wallpapering made easy

It is quicker and easier to paper a 1/24 room than one in 1/12. Make a paper pattern of each wall from used photocopy paper or stiff brown paper, and use it as a template to cut the wallpaper pieces. You can cover two walls with one piece, so that there is no need to match any pattern at the corner, but to avoid problems, use a separate piece for a wall with a doorway or window, or a fireplace. Textured paper can be butted together at corners, where an overlap would form a ridge. The join will be unnoticeable because of the raised finish.

One that worked! The wallpaper used here is a giftwrap design which achieves the right effect in this unusual room (see page 80 for finished setting). The ceiling 'painting' is taken from a museum postcard.

The door frame has yet to be added, and a dado rail will cover the join between the textured paper and the Chinese decorations above. The fireplace is of cast resin. Note that the marble hearth and surround will be glued to the wall and floor before the fireplace is fitted.

Paste or glue

Test which adhesive works best before pasting on unusual papers. Wallpaper paste will not work well on some textured or handmade papers. Paste a small test piece on to card and allow to dry before checking to see whether it has stuck firmly. Thick papers and card may need a trail of general-purpose glue around the edges in addition to paste all over, to prevent them curling up.

Never use paper glue on magazine cuttings as it will cause wrinkles when it dries. Fix magazine cuttings on to thin white card with general-purpose glue before gluing that, in turn, into the house.

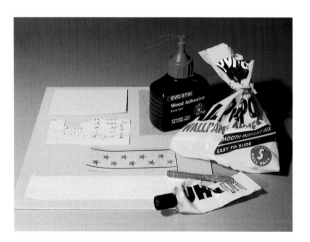

Test different adhesives on paper samples.

It is worth sizing the walls first if you are using dolls' house wallpaper. Brush on a thin coat of wallpaper paste and leave until dry to the touch. Paste the paper, making sure that you cover the corners well. Smooth down by pressing all over with a pad of toilet tissues. Do not rub. Rubbing may cause wrinkles or even tears in thin paper.

Ways with wallpaper

■ Use leftover scraps of wallpaper to line shelves and drawers or to liven up an alcove in a plainly painted room.
■ Or make a lampshade.

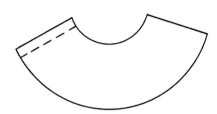

1 A rounded shape is very simple.

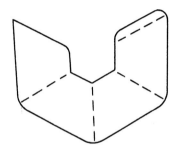

2 The lampshade topping the standard lamp in the tea room (see page 90) is made by cutting and folding wallpaper.

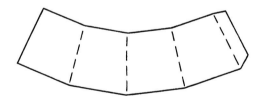

3 Another useful shape suitable for a table lamp.

Use a pearl bead, or in the case of this lampshade, which has a wider opening at the top, a small pearl button, to support the shade. Attach the bead or button to the lampbase with glue or Blu-tack.

(The patterns are drawn in a suitable size so that they can be traced.)

Trompe l'oeil

Magazine illustrations and museum postcards can be cut down to provide wall paintings and pictured effects which will give a three-dimensional appearance. They work best if used at the back of a staircase, where they will be partly obscured by the balusters, allowing an intriguing glimpse of a 'painted' scene or fresco (see page 75).

The postcard sections shown here were all considered as trompe l'oeil effects for the Georgian house. The distant doorway in the centre of the picture was selected to use at the end of the hall, to create a perspective effect.

Using card on walls and floors

Walls

Museum and exhibition postcards depicting painted panels and textiles can also be used to simulate hand-painted wallpaper panels. Make sure that you buy more than enough cards for your planned interior, as it may not be possible to buy more later.

Flooring

Stone, marble and tiled floors can be simulated using card. In 1/24, the area covered is so small that this will give a good impression. Cut with a craft knife and raised-edge metal ruler.

Wooden floors can also be simulated (see page 100), but 1/24 iron-on planking looks more realistic and is easy to fit (follow the maker's instructions). The wooden planks should be ironed on to a card template of the floor which can be glued in place after trimming for a perfect fit (see page 63). Plasticized sheets of 'wood' flooring are also available, to cut and put down in one piece.

To fit card floors

Cut a paper pattern of the floor and use as a template to cut the card. To make the template, start with a piece of stiff paper slightly larger than the floor size, crease then trim the edges to fit. Mark and trim round a chimney breast and extend into any doorway. Check that the pattern fits perfectly before cutting the card from it. Use card of similar thickness for adjacent rooms, so that there will be no need to cover the joins in doorways.

Order of decoration

Decorating a 1/24 house follows the same principles as one in 1/12. In practical terms, painting or papering a wall is the same procedure. But small rooms may look their best with simplified schemes – here, life is made easier for the decorator, as over elaboration will not be effective.

For the beginner, it can be difficult to decide where to start. I discussed practical decoration in detail in an earlier book (*A Beginner's Guide to the Dolls' House Hobby*), so for new miniaturists, here is a brief reminder of a suggested order of work, which includes a number of options. Hobbyists who have decorated dolls' houses before will be familiar with at least some of these procedures.

A house which needs no exterior decoration, and which will appeal to anyone who appreciates the beauty of well-polished wood. It is made in reclaimed Victorian pine, or can be ordered in a variety of English hardwoods. Resembling an antique dolls' house, it fastens with a brass lock and key.

Exterior decoration

How much decoration do you want to do yourself? This all depends on how much realism you want and whether you enjoy using modelling materials. If you do, there are many ways to customize a basic house by adding various forms of cladding (see page 50).

Three Yorkshire houses. The colours are well-chosen and make each house distinctive.

Twenty steps to basic decoration

Preparation
1 Smooth over both exterior and interior surfaces with fine glasspaper.
2 Fill any cracks and leave to dry. For this purpose, interior filler is better than wood filler, as it is finer. Sand again.
3 Make sure that the house is free of dust before you begin painting. If possible use a suction cleaner with a fine nozzle attachment.
4 Paint both exterior and interior walls with quick-drying primer or undercoat.
5 Apply two coats of emulsion to the ceilings. One coat is sufficient if you plan any special treatment later.

Exterior decoration
6 Paint the exterior walls and the roof.
7 Paint window and door frames.
8 Paint the front door. Door furniture (knob, letterbox, knocker) can be fitted at this stage, or after the decorations are completed.

Interior design
9 Fit any lighting.*
10 Make and site chimney breasts.*
11 Fit fireplaces.*
12 Make any required additions to staircase (balusters, newel posts, side panels).*
13 Fit flooring.
14 Fit internal doors.*

Interior decoration
15 Paint walls in your chosen colours.
16 Wallpaper walls as an alternative to paint.
17 Add wallpaper borders.*

Fittings
18 Fit door frames.
19 Cut, paint and fit skirtings, cornice and dado rail or picture rail.*
20 Cut and fit window glazing and internal window frames.
(* = optional)

You may not wish to plan and carry out elaborate schemes, and there is a lot to be said for the straightforward approach, especially if you have limited time for your hobby. A plain, painted finish will look attractive, be hard-wearing, and if your main interest is in interior decoration and furnishing, this will leave you more time to concentrate on what you enjoy most.

Colour schemes

Colour is very much a matter of personal choice, but the style of house should influence your decisions. The facade should reflect its period and be decorated accordingly if it is to look its best. For beginners, and as a reminder to the more experienced, here is a guide to exterior decoration.

John Nash designed several versions of this Italianate villa, finished in stucco, which can be reproduced with a simple painted finish. The galleried arcade is an attractive feature which could be used as an orangery (see page 109) or for outdoor seating.

Suitable colours and exterior finishes on period houses

Period		Finishes
Tudor/Jacobean (16th/early 17th century)	Walls	Plaster with half timbering. White, ochre, pale pink or apricot infilling
	Timber	Stained. Use walnut stain, which is warmer than light oak, to complement pale-coloured plaster. Wood stain or varnish doors and window surrounds. (Blackened timbers were a Victorian fashion and look striking with white plaster.)
	Roof	Stone tiles or simulated thatch
Georgian (18th century)	Walls	Painted as stucco for a town house, using stone-coloured paint. A small Georgian cottage might be pink, pale blue or cream
	Roof	Grey or russet slates, or paint
	Paintwork	'Georgian' white (off-white) for window frames and surrounds
	Front door	Dark green, black or white
	Railings	Today's Georgian house usually has black painted railings, but a dark bronze-green is more authentic
Victorian town house (19th century)	Walls	Brick; use plasticized sheets or individual brick slips
	Roof	Grey slate, or grey paint
	Additions	Brass door furniture and letter box
	Front door	Black or deep blue

Period		Finishes
Victorian country house (19th century)	Walls	Red brick
	Roof	Slate grey
	Additions	Bargeboards on gable ends
		A clock tower or a turret
	Front door	Dark green
Edwardian (early 20th century)	Walls	Brick
	Roof	Red slates or paint
	Paintwork	White
	Additions	Balcony or veranda, porch
		Mock half-timbers on gable ends
	Front door	Stained glass panels
1930s–40s	Walls	Brick or pebble dash; to represent pebble dash glue on glasspaper rough side out and paint grey/stone
	Roof	Red or grey slates
	Paintwork	Mid-green. (Front door can be green, white, or stained as oak.)
	Additions	Letter box
		Stained glass panels over front door and in top lights of the windows
		Porch with red quarry tiles
Country cottage	Walls	Colourwashed white, pink, blue or creamy yellow; occasionally Suffolk pink
		Or stone clad
	Roof	Thatch or slate
	Paintwork	White or colour
	Additions	Porch

Interior decoration

The easiest way to decorate internal walls is to apply two coats of emulsion paint. You can enjoy choosing colour schemes without the necessity for pasting wallpaper and matching pattern repeats. It is advisable to begin with a coat of white, quick-drying undercoat (see page 32), so that any marks from the wood will not show through later.

It is worth looking at a variety of papers and trompe l'oeil ideas in the rooms for which they are intended before coming to a final decision on which to use.

Choosing colours

Using an authentic colour in a period house can be fun, but be wary of using very bright shades, which in 1/24 might dominate a small room. You need to be able to see the furniture without being dazzled by the background.

I do not advise that you use neutral colours throughout, as this could look dull. However some 'historic' colours are very startling – the popular Georgian shade known as 'smalt' is an extremely vivid deep blue, and few people would choose to decorate their dolls' house rooms in 'Mummy Pink', or to go to the other extreme, 'Mouse' or 'Drab' – all names of authentic eighteenth-century paint shades which are again being produced today.

Edwardian and Art Deco colours are often too strong for miniature homes. Instead choose a similar, but slightly less startling shade from a modern paint range. For cottage or Tudor walls, both outside and in, off-white, any of the ochre shades from pale cream to deep yellow, or a sandy pink, are authentic. In a modern-style dolls' house, you can choose your favourite colours and may be able to make use of leftover paints from your own home decoration.

Suitable colours and features for period interiors

Period		Colours/Features
Tudor/Jacobean (16th/early 17th century)	Walls	Colourwashed in ochre, white or terracotta or oak panelling (natural or dark)
	Ceilings	Oak beams (natural or dark)
	Floors	Stone, simulated in card (see page 53) or made from modelling clay, or oak planking
	Features	Open fireplace; log fires (see page 55), stencilled decoration
Georgian (18th century)	Walls	Adam blue or green, 'pearl' (see page 84) for the best rooms or wallpaper
	Features	Ceiling centrepieces (see page 84), skirtings, dado rails and cornice
	Floors	Unpolished wooden planking
Victorian (19th century)	Walls	Wallpaper
	Paintwork	White or wood stain
	Features	Elaborate fireplaces in marble (dolls' house versions are in cast resin, see pages 78–81), curtains and/or blinds, inner lace curtains
	Additions	Clutter – ornaments, footstools, occasional tables, firescreens
Charles Rennie Mackintosh style (early 20th century)	Walls and ceilings	White, stencilled decorations on walls
	Flooring	Plain, pale carpeting
	Paintwork	White, occasionally very dark, almost black, but white looks better in dolls' houses
	Features	Gesso (plaster) wall plaques black, high-backed chairs, stained glass where possible

Period		Colours/Features
Edwardian (early 20th century)	Walls	Floral wallpapers, borders and friezes
	Flooring	Polished wooden floors with carpet square
	Paintwork	White, or stained medium oak
	Additions	Mirror above fireplace, grate with tiled surround and elaborate mantelpiece sometimes incorporating shelves on either side
1930s–40s	Kitchens	Green and cream was the standard colour scheme
	Bedrooms	Often pink
	Lounge	Cream-washed walls with green, floral or fawn soft furnishings. For the wealthy, an entirely pale room in shades of white or cream
	Bathroom	Tiled walls
	Floors	Medium-oak floor surround and patterned carpet square, or fitted carpet. Quarry tiles in the kitchen
	Paintwork	Cream, or wood-grained finish
	Accessories	Standard lamps, hearthrug wall lights, ceramic flying ducks on the wall, Art Deco statuettes

Troubleshooting

There are a few specific areas of decoration which seem to cause difficulties. Here are some potential problems and their solutions. (For more detailed instructions, see later sections in Part Two.)

Problem 1 Painting exterior window frames

Solution

Paint the exterior wall first and leave to dry thoroughly. Then fix masking tape on to the wall around each window before painting the frame. I recommend forty-eight hours drying time for the paint on the facade before applying masking tape.

Window frames are ready-fitted to this house. Before painting, remove the front door by unscrewing the hinges.

Problem 2 Decorating the outside of a half-timbered house.

Solution
This is a similar problem, but the sequence should be reversed. Stain or varnish the timbers before you deal with the walls. Then add cladding cut to fit the spaces and cover up any smudges of stain on the walls. To simulate a plastered finish, see page 50.

Problem 3 Painting or papering around a fixed-in staircase.

Solution
Most 1/24 dolls' house staircases can be taken out for decoration. If it is fixed in place, you can deal with it, slowly and with patience. Varnishing should always be done before painting. If the stair treads and hand rail are to be stained or varnished, do this first. When dry, cover the stairs with masking tape before painting the balusters.

Problem 4 Painting low ceilings in small rooms.

Solution
Cut the paintbrush handle to about 4in long so that you can reach inside the room. Sponge-tipped applicators (sold in packets, for applying eye make-up) can also be useful in tight corners and they are cheap enough to be disposable. Check the applicator periodically during use to make sure that the sponge tip does not work loose and fall off.

Problem 5 Order of interior decoration.

Solution
As a general rule, if anything might drip on to the surface below, paint it first – for example, ceilings before walls. Even though you may mask the lower surface, there is always the possibility of a paint drip or smudge, which can then be removed before the next stage without spoiling an already painted or varnished surface.

Bronze-green is a good colour for balusters and handrail on a Georgian staircase. As an alter-native, use Georgian white (off-white).

5 *Lighting*

Electric lighting creates a magical effect in any dolls' house, and 1/24 is no exception, but it is even more fiddly to get just right. If you plan to light your house, it is best to work out a detailed lighting plan at the start; miniature lighting suppliers can provide a booklet containing detailed instructions or a lighting kit tailored to your needs.

Period lighting installed in an Oxfordshire cottage (see picture at top of page 66) gives a welcoming impression.

The copper tape system is the most popular – the flat conductors can be concealed under the floor covering or below ceilings and taken through to the lighting points. You will need an adaptor, which can be purchased from the lighting supplier, a railway modeller shop or an electrical shop stocking television and radio equipment.

The adaptor may have switches for different voltages, so that it can be used with either 6 or 12 volt bulbs.

A well-lit interior makes it possible to see every detail of the woodwork in this period home.

For low, atmospheric lighting, which is particularly suitable for very tiny buildings or two-room cottages, use 6 volt bulbs – screw-in bulbs and holders with two solder wires to be attached to the wiring can be obtained from stockists as above. Screw-in bulbs (also available in 9 and 12 volt) can be changed easily when necessary.

For stronger lighting, 12 volt is needed, and for this, 12 volt grain-of-wheat bulbs are standard. These are, however, more difficult to replace if they burn out. Check our procedures in your lighting instructions booklet before you come to a decision.

Miniaturists will find stands specializing in lighting at major miniatures shows. An expert will be available to give explanations and advice on the best system for your project.

6 *Furnishing*

Whether you are furnishing a whole house or a single room, it is best to arrange the essential furniture first before thinking about accessories. These can be added gradually to complete the setting.

Furnishing a dolls' house room requires balanced judgement. The secret of successful real-life interior decoration is to know when to stop, to judge when the addition of one extra picture or small table will ruin the effect – and the same applies in miniature rooms.

Two partly-furnished rooms in a Charles Rennie Mackintosh interior based on Hill House, near Glasgow. There is space for more pieces in these rooms but care will be needed in arranging additions to show them to advantage.

A gorgeous Venetian Palace is the perfect setting for gilded Louis XIV furniture. This remarkable miniature Hall of Mirrors represents months of work by the miniaturist.

The ardent collector may be tempted to accumulate more and more miniatures, on the principle that there is always room for more, but it is a good idea to pause and take a critical look at intervals while you furnish a room. It may be perfect with one or two items removed rather than with another added.

This applies especially to 1/24 scale; the rooms are so tiny that they do not need a great deal of furniture to create a good impression. Leave some space between the miniatures you display, so that they can be seen and appreciated.

A cosy corner in a Victorian kitchen.

There are exceptions to this rule. Kitchens and nurseries, and in particular late Victorian rooms, seem able to accommodate a huge number of gadgets, ornaments, food or toys before they look overfilled. The classical Georgian room, on the other hand, was sparsely furnished, with most of the pieces arranged neatly against the walls. Tudor and Jacobean houses had very little furniture, and what there was, was essential – to sit on, to lie on, or to eat off.

The cost of furnishing

Simple furniture will be inexpensive, but not all 1/24 miniatures are cheaper than their 1/12 counterparts. I have come across dismayed makers of exquisite 1/24 pieces who have been told that their prices should be half the cost of a similar item in 1/12.

Hand-carved ropework is an exceptional feature on this double-ended sofa. The upholstery is covered in fine, striped silk and there are two bolster-shaped cushions. To be workable in this size, the fabric used must be both delicate and flexible.

There is certainly a small saving on materials which can be passed on to the customer, but very often, if the piece is elaborate, it will have taken as long or even longer to make than the larger equivalent. If it is finely carved or gilded, the time taken in making will be reflected in the price. Tiny needlework, too, can take much longer to make and finish properly than when worked on a coarser fabric.

A well-finished rocking chair supplied ready for painting or varnishing.

However, in general, furnishing in 1/24 is economical compared with 1/12. Outlay on materials for home-made items will be small – soft furnishings will need little fabric, card can sometimes be used instead of wood. Plain, well-made furniture is inexpensive, and can be varnished or painted in your choice of finish. For modern interiors, 1/25 scale plastic kits of television sets or audio equipment are easy to assemble and paint, and look realistic.

Quick-reference furniture style guide

Tudor

An oak table made from 400-year-old oak salvaged from the Windsor Castle fire, one of only two miniature tables made.

Georgian

A plain mahogany table was the epitome of good taste in the early Georgian period. All the detail is in the carved pedestal and legs.

Victorian

The Victorian prie-dieu chair was designed for prayer and often richly upholstered. This miniature version is beautifully finished and would make a decorative addition to the bedroom or drawing room.

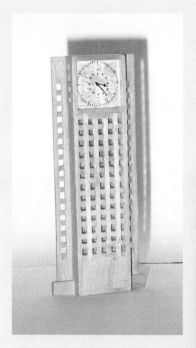

Mackintosh

This unusual longcase clock in lattice-work wood could only be a Mackintosh design. The miniature is copied from one used in the Willow Tea Rooms in Glasgow.

Art Deco

A distinctive set of Art Deco dining table and chairs. The maker prefers to use a close-grained wood when working in 1/24, but in this instance the colours of sycamore and rosewood are essential for the style. Extra care is needed when selecting wood to avoid knots or blemishes which might spoil the clean effect.

1920s/30s onwards

An instantly recognizable design classic, the Lloyd Loom chair was first made in 1922 and during the 1930s there was generally at least one in every middle-class home. The miniaturist has scaled down the original materials used commercially – brown paper-covered wire – and uses fine wire and crochet thread to make this exact reproduction.

7 *Dolls*

A Victorian mother and two delightful children. Tiny, beautifully dressed dolls which can be posed in a really lifelike manner, make a homely scene in even the smallest dolls' house room.

Dolls are not obligatory in today's hobby. It depends on whether your priority is interior decoration and furnishing or to have fun with a house that looks lived in. Your decision whether or not to include dolls may also be influenced by the views of other members of your family, particularly if you have children or grandchildren.

Professional miniaturists make costumed dolls to suit any period style, from exquisitely dressed Tudor ladies and gentlemen to casual modern-style people. Kits are also available to make and dress your own dolls, even in this small scale. Heads are usually of porcelain, with soft bodies and wired arms and legs so that the dolls can be posed.

A Regency couple dressed in the height of fashion. The lady's high-waisted striped silk dress is covered by a matching lace-trimmed coat, while the gentleman wears buckskin trousers, a waisted coat and an elaborate cravat.

A fairy-like creature made from papier-mâché as one of the dancers in a ballroom scene. She is a miniaturist's fantasy from the top of her elaborate wig to the tip of her dainty sandal.

Tudor gentlefolk and their retainers.

This doll was dressed by the maker, but is also available as a kit to assemble and dress to suit any setting.

Men's dress in the time of Charles II was extraordinarily elaborate. The cavalier is dressed in lace-trimmed velvet in exquisite detail, and carries a matching hat with feathers.

Part Two
Decorative styles

On the following pages, the decoration of two complete houses, one Tudor and one Georgian, is discussed stage-by-stage, and further ideas are given for shops, period and modern houses and a series of imaginative room box settings. Instructions are given to explain the simplest and most economical ways to achieve effects, with further suggestions on how to tackle more elaborate schemes which you might care to try out.

Pictures and diagrams illustrate a variety of working methods, which will be useful whatever style of house you plan to decorate.

Even in 1/24, this miniature building is six feet long. All the wood is recycled from old roof timbers, and there are 13,000 tiles individually cut and fitted to the roof.

8 *Decorating a Tudor house*

Tudor houses are available in all shapes and sizes, most based to some extent on real houses, although a few craftspeople produce the most engaging imagined homes.

One typical Tudor style is the Wealden house, instantly recognizable with a central hall and a bay at either end. Originally, the hall would have had an open fire, an external chimney breast, fireplace and hearth were added later. Wealden houses are popular with makers, and there is plenty of choice for hobbyists.

This version of a Wealden house demonstrates additions made in the later Tudor period to include brick facing on the original hall. Like the brick additions, the close-studded timbers at either end show later work. This dolls' house was made by a hobbyist in three separate sections. Although wood has been used to provide the timbering, the walls and roof are made of foamboard and sheet cladding has been added.

Pictured here are three versions of the Wealden house, each by a different maker.

Right **A professionally-made model which is still a Wealden house, although like many such buildings that still survive, it has been plastered over. Its origins are instantly recognizable by the jettied front and massive chimney.**

Below **This view of a house under construction shows the amount of timber used in the traditional method of building a Wealden house. It is copied from an actual building now at the Weald and Downland Open Air Museum in Sussex.**

Below **An extended version of the small mill used as an example of Tudor decoration in this section. Real brick and stone cladding have been added. The roof features real slates and even the mill yard is stone clad. The mill was a very important building in Tudor times, when bread was a staple part of the diet. Without the mill, people would have starved.**

Tudor exterior decoration

Walls

Exterior walls can be treated in a variety of ways, but the principle is the same whether the house is small or large. Deal with the half-timbering first, because although you can paint over stain if necessary, you cannot stain or varnish over paint.

One version of the Tudor house seen today has blackened timbers and white infill. Originally the wood would have been oak in its natural pale state – the fashion for

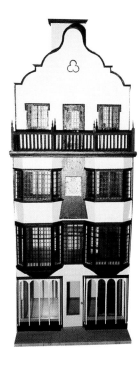

An exact replica of a remarkable house in the cathedral close at Exeter. It has a distinct maritime feeling, appropriate to its situation in a once thriving port. The miniature was produced as one of a limited-edition kit and can also be supplied fully finished.

a paper pattern of each space, using a thin paper which can be creased along the beam edges initially, and then transfer the shape to a firmer paper to use as a template. Make adjustments to the template so that it exactly fits the space.

Paint a sheet of thin textured card with emulsion paint in your chosen colour: cream, any shade of ochre or pink are most suitable. When dry, cut out the shapes using the templates and glue the textured paper in place. This method is time consuming and needs patience, but it works well and the plaster-look finish will be perfect.

blackening was introduced in Victorian times, but has remained popular and looks striking. To decorate a house in this way, use a very dark woodstain (if necessary applying two coats) and an off-white rather than pure white for the infill (see below).

The timbers on most Tudor houses today are in their natural weathered oak and I chose this option for the mill house. A walnut shade gives a better effect than light oak as it provides sufficient contrast with infill.

Infill has been colourwashed to suggest weathering.

When choosing stain or varnish, getting the colour right is what matters, not what the shade is called on the maker's list. Look at the shade card colours rather than the name of the wood the colour represents.

Painting the infill

On a tiny house, the spaces between the wooden timbers can be very small and almost impossible to paint without smudging on to the stained wood. The best method is to make

Brick infill

Brick infill is another variation, and you may choose to add at least some brick facing to the exterior, provided that the spaces between the timbers are square or rectangular (see page 51). The quickest method is to use sheets of brick cladding, which can be cut to fit the spaces

Brick slips have been added below the ground floor windows on this sturdy yeoman's house. When completed, the russet-coloured slate roof will add to the realistic effect.

between timbers as above. For complete realism, use brick slips. This is more time consuming but well worth the effort. Easy-to-follow instructions are provided by the supplier, who will also provide a cement-based adhesive, or you can use tile grout.

Stone cladding

Stone cladding is also an option, using sheet cladding or making individual stone slabs and painting (see page 54).

Textured, painted stone represents the variations in colour of natural stone after four hundred years of exposure to the elements. Note that the larger slabs are near the doorway, to impress, while smaller, rubble stone is used as infill in the narrower spaces between the structural timbers. The undulating roof is a pleasure to look at.

The roof

Roofing slate is also available both as sheet cladding or individual slates. If using real slate, start at the bottom and work up to the top of the roof, overlapping each row to cover about a third of the slate underneath. Stagger the slates, as on a real roof, using a half-slate at the ends of rows where necessary.

On a very small house the simplest method of roofing often works best. Satinwood paint in a cheerful russet colour is used on this small roof.

Make a mill race

The mill has a mill wheel which can be turned round. A mill race (running water effect) is fun to make and adds realism. This method can also be adapted to make a small stream or a flat pond for a garden setting.

Method

1 Cut a card base to fit the shape required – in this case, under the planking and around the wheel. The wheel is removable, but to make sure that there is enough space left for it to

After texturing and painting, the card used for the mill race is realistically watery.

turn, it is best to cut two pieces of card to fit together under the centre of the wheel, the lowest point. Cut two separate pieces, it is easier to try out for size and slip in place when completed.

2 To make a stream, measure the length and width required and cut a length of card with gently curving edges to suit your garden setting.

3 Mix some interior filler with a little water and PVA wood glue and cover the card base, making a raised shape to resemble the flow of the water. When set, paint with a green/brown mix of model enamel, to make a muddy colour.

4 Varnish with three coats of gloss varnish. After the second coat, paint white flecks to resemble foam and spray using gloss white paint. Paint on in a swirling motion, feathering lightly. Then add the final coat of varnish.

The finished 'race' effect below the mill wheel, which can be turned with a fingertip.

For a gentle, trickling stream, you need only a little white; before the final coat of varnish. Add some tiny slivers of grass or greenish raffia to represent weeds floating in the water. For a garden pond, omit the white flecks.

Tudor interior decoration

Basic decoration is a simple matter in a Tudor house, and if internal timbers and ceiling beams are provided, there is little you need to do initially beyond the application of a coat of off-white emulsion. It may be helpful to use the card method suggested for the exterior walls.

This delightful Tudor house features a concealed doorway to a secret room. It is fully lit to show the beauty of the wooden panelling and inglenook fireplaces.

Many makers omit interior timbers, leaving you to add beams if you wish after decoration; use stripwood, stained before gluing in place. Cut the lengths slightly crooked for realism. In at least some of the rooms, walls can be assumed to have been plastered over, and in a tiny house, some plain walls will make it appear more spacious. Colourwash in pale yellow ochre or pale pink, with perhaps one wall or a ceiling in a deeper Suffolk pink.

If your house has many rooms, you might like to add wooden panelling somewhere. Panelling is available in cast resin, which can be stained by applying three coats of timber

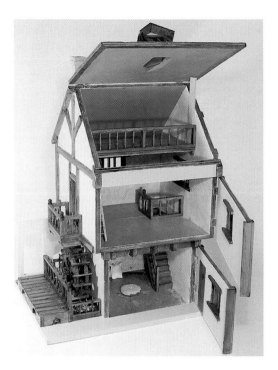

A lift-up roof and ceiling, colourwashed in Suffolk pink to contrast with the stone walls below.

dressing, e.g. Cuprinol. Stain wooden panelling with woodstain and finish with a coat of satin or matt varnish, depending on the degree of shine you prefer.

Stencilling

Originally, Tudor interior walls were often covered with colourful decoration; most wall paintings have long since disappeared, but some paintings will add colour and interest. You need not paint a whole scene – a few fragments will give an impression of authenticity. Miniature stencils can be useful here. Brass stencils are available in a wide range of designs, including borders of trailing leaves. Flowers and leaves were often included in early wall paintings.

Tape the stencil in place with masking tape. Use either paint and a size 0 paintbrush or waterproof crayons, well sharpened so that the point is easy to get into the smallest spaces on the stencil. If it is difficult to reach into the

room, cut a piece of thin card the exact size of the wall to be stencilled and paint it the same colour as the rest of the room. Add the design before gluing the piece of card in place.

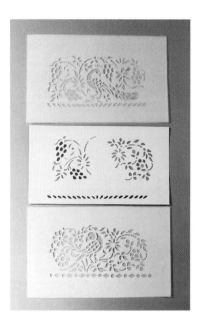

Part of an inexpensive plastic stencil, made in China. Such stencils are available from many gift and souvenir shops in a variety of delicate designs. They measure around 2⅜in (60mm) deep by 4in (100mm) long and include a useful border design which can be repeated around a room.

Flooring

Simulate a stone floor in card, which can look very realistic on a small floor area.

Cut out a paper pattern first from stiff paper (used photocopying paper or stiff brown paper is economical). Check the fit carefully and make any adjustments before you cut the actual floor. Colour the front edge of the card to match the surface with a felt-tip pen to avoid a white line showing up later. Cover the reverse side of the card with general-purpose glue, making sure that there is plenty around the edges. Wait until the glue is tacky before pressing the card into place, to avoid any seepage on to the top surface.

Stone floors are suitable in many other situations besides Tudor houses. Country cottages and Georgian and Victorian houses may all have stone floors.

Providing you can find a good pictured representation of stone on card, this is the simplest option to take (see below right), but there are other ways to simulate stone. Make use of leftover materials from full-size decoration for realism. The following methods can also be used to provide stone facing for cottages (see pictures on pages 65 and 70) or to make garden paths (see page 111).

- Plasticized sheets of stone cladding can be used in the same way as brick and slate.
- Paint the floor with textured paint (from craft and decorating shops).
- Tile adhesive is a good off-white/grey colour with some variation, and does not need painting. Spread over the floor, score with a knife or a metal spatula to mark out stone slabs and leave to dry.
- Car body filler can be used similarly, then painted in random colours.
- Modelling clay makes good stone slabs. Roll out thinly, score and paint as above. Glue in place with PVA wood glue.

Make your own flour sacks

Flour sacks are essential for a mill, but also have many other uses. It is economical to make your own sacks for garden and shop use too. Use any fine, linen-type fabric to reproduce sacking in this scale – an old linen handkerchief is ideal. The flour sacks are off-white, but sacks for shop or garden use should be darker. Stain pale material by dipping in cold, weak tea or coffee before making up.

Wood and tile floors in an unfinished Tudor house. The maker is building up the tiled floor to show the effects of wear and age.

The plastered walls inside the mill house are of rough textured handmade paper in a greyish-white, to suit a working building. The 'stone' floor is made of card. A few flour sacks help to create atmosphere.

Method

1 Cut a strip of fabric approximately 1½in (38mm) wide by 3½in (89mm) high. (Exact size is not crucial). Turn in ¼in (6mm) on all edges. Tack turned-in hem in place.

Diagram 1

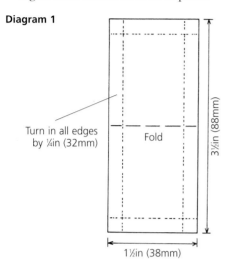

Turn in all edges by ¼in (32mm)

Fold

3½in (88mm)

1½in (38mm)

2 Fold in half and crease firmly. Sew sides together neatly, or glue if preferred.

3 Fill it three-quarters full with couscous or bird seed to give a realistic look and feel.

Diagram 2

Pinch together in centre and twist at corners.

4 Sew or glue tops together neatly. Pinch together in the top centre, twist firmly at corners and add a stitch or dab of glue to hold the twist together.

Make a log fire

If your house boasts an inglenook fireplace provide a good fire. Ready-made log fires can be purchased fitted with flickering lights, but they may not fit your space. It is easy to make a log fire which can glow with warmth, even without electricity. Gather up some small twigs next time you go for a walk, or look round the garden.

Method

1 Cut a card base a fraction smaller than the length of the inside of the fireplace and ¼in (6mm) less than the depth. Cut the front edges unevenly.

Diagram 3

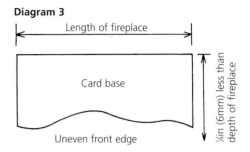

Length of fireplace

Card base

¼in (6mm) less than depth of fireplace

Uneven front edge

2 To build up the fire so that it shows to advantage from the front, cut a thin length of wood strip or card about ¼in (6mm) wide by ⅛in (3mm) thick to fit along the back of the card base, and glue it in place.

3 Remember that a wood fire produces plenty of ash. Spread a layer of interior filler over the base, making it a bit bumpy. When this is set, paint it with textured paint or ash grey model enamel and add a few flecks of black. Glue the 'logs' on top.

Diagram 4

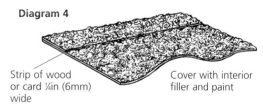

Strip of wood or card ¼in (6mm) wide

Cover with interior filler and paint

4 Finally, paint part of the logs with ash grey and some black, plus a red/orange mix on the undersides of some of the logs which are in view.

Keep some spare twigs to make a log pile by the fire.

The finished log fire before fitting into the inglenook fireplace.

Furnishing a Tudor house

Tudor houses had very little furniture. Even grand homes often possessed only one four-poster bed, a chair for the master and a similar, smaller one for his lady. Everyone else had to make do with truckle beds and benches, and servants sat and slept where they could find a space. There might be a cupboard (known as a hutch) and a chest or two for storage (see pages 79 and page 80).

Gleaming pewter candle sconces, plates and mugs, flagons and dishes will make the house look lived in. Tapestries can be hung on the walls to add warmth, and replicas of swords and shields can also decorate walls.

Taken from the French millefleurs design, this tapestry is not handworked but is reproduced photographically. When hung on a dolls' house wall it looks impressive.

An atmospheric Tudor interior.

A suit of armour and weapons are the ultimate decorative addition to a Tudor house of grand proportions, as visitors to stately homes of this period will know. Pewter in a plainer guise is used for the tankards and dishes on the table, left unpolished to show use.

Make your own tapestry cushions

You could work your own tapestry, but in such a small scale this is probably too much of a challenge for any but the most expert needle-woman (or man). Fake tapestries can look much like the real thing, once hung on a wall.

If you are fond of canvas work embroidery, work a small piece of Florentine stitch for a cushion to make a stool or settle look more comfortable. Use fine linen or Aida and work upright stitches over two threads in a zigzag, using enough strands of embroidery cotton to fill the holes.

Red, green and gold is a good colour combination to brighten a Tudor house. Many patterns are possible with Florentine stitch, and the one shown is the easiest to work. More elaborate stitch patterns will be found in any needlework stitch guide but the more complicated variations will not show to advantage in 1/24.

Alternate rows of stitches should be in a different colour, as shown. Once you have worked the first row to set the pattern, follow the same sequence until your work is large enough. Turn in the edges and stitch neatly to a backing of thicker fabric.

A complete set of hangings is not needed for this wonderfully carved bed, which is based on an early design where wood was used rather than fabric to keep out draughts. A coverlet and side curtains will be required.

Make hangings for a four-poster bed

Most people like to include a four-poster bed in a Tudor dolls' house, and there are a number of arrangements which can be used for the hangings, depending on whether the bedposts are plain or carved. The usual features are a valance at the base and a canopy at the top, unless a carved wooden one is provided. Curtains at the corners can be looped back with cords (made from gilt giftwrap string or plaited embroidery silk) to display the coverlet and any carving on the headboard.

The valance can run all the way round (see diagram 1) or be divided at the corners to show the bedposts (see diagram 2).

Exquisite hand-embroidered hangings taken from a Tudor design complete this plain oak bed.

To make a valance

Method 1

Measure the height of the bed base (not the height of the four-poster bed frame). Cut a length of fabric twice this measurement plus ¾in (19mm) for the turnings and long enough to fit along the sides and foot of bed with 1½in (38mm) turnings at the ends. Fold in half lengthwise and press.

Turn in and stitch the top edges and ends neatly. Attach double-sided adhesive tape to the sides of the bed base and press the valance in place.

Diagram 1

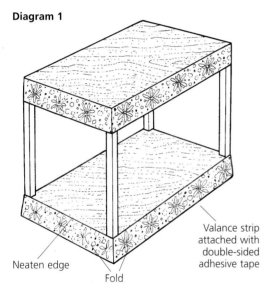

Neaten edge
Fold
Valance strip attached with double-sided adhesive tape

Method 2

Divide the fabric for the valance into three lengths to fit between the bedposts, remembering to allow extra for turnings at both ends of each length, and attach as before.

Diagram 2

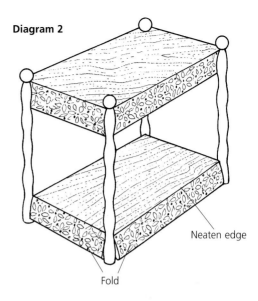

Neaten edge
Fold

Quick tip

Avoid sewing by using furnishing braid to make the valance and canopy. To minimize bulk, do not hem the ends but neaten with a smear of general-purpose glue applied with a wooden cocktail stick.

A canopy

A strip of braid or fabric with the top edges sewn neatly together, to form a canopy, can, again, be attached in one piece or in separate sections to leave carved posts exposed. Fix on with double-sided adhesive tape.

Hangings and coverlet can be made from thin velvet, embroidered or plain linen. Red striped 'worsted' was also a popular choice and can be simulated in striped cotton. The coverlet should overhang the valance to cover the top edges.

9 *Tudor for modern living*

The completed interior of the mill house in its updated mode. A small Tudor house can be treated in an individual way while keeping the period features.

The completed interior of the mill house in its updated mode. A small Tudor house can be treated in an individual way while keeping the period features.

sympathetic updating, with some original features still in evidence. Some modern furniture will add spice to a Tudor interior.

Decorating the little mill house was discussed in detail in the preceding section, and apart from the flooring in the upper part of the building, the interior decoration has not changed for its new use. It is still a working building, as the ground floor is now used as a country potter's workshop, while the upstairs features a colourful, modern sitting room/kitchen and a galleried bedroom.

Such a combination provides many opportunities to make furniture and fittings. A working pottery should not be tidy, and is always fairly heavily spattered with clay. Shelves to stack unfinished pots, a potter's wheel and a small kiln, tables, and shelves made from any odd pieces of wood which come to hand, are essential. A small sink is needed too and a few jugs and bowls.

Many Tudor houses are still in use today, adapted as comfortable modern homes. Although the exterior will have changed little, this arrangement is a chance to explore

The artfully clay-spattered pottery in this picture is based on some real-life examples. The miniature potter specializes in making plant pots, and the finished wares are displayed at the front of his workshop to attract passing trade.

Make a potter's workshop

You will need:

- **A potter's wheel.** Use a button, preferably with grooves in concentric circles, and mount it on a small bead. The wooden base can be triangular or rectangular in shape. Cut the pieces from balsa or stripwood, glue together, and mount on a small table. Sponge on a watered-down mix of grey/white emulsion.
- **Shelves.** Make from short lengths of thin stripwood. Paint as above.
- **A kiln.** Paint a plastic bottle cap with two coats of metallic paint such as Metalcote, and burnish.
- **Mounds of prepared 'clay'.** Mix some interior filler to a stiff paste. Add a drop of paint for terracotta clay. Shape into small mounds; these can be kept ready for work on a table or shelf topped with a slate slab.
- **A lidded doughbox for storage.** Paint a ready-made doughbox with a watered down mix of grey/white emulsion.

In the upstairs sitting room, all is 1990s Conran style. The Aga provides both warmth and cooking facilities. Plain wooden chairs and tables can be limed in modern style by wiping over with cream-coloured emulsion to give a streaky effect. The television, made from a 1/25 scale American kit, is mounted on a round table so that it can be swivelled for family viewing.

The Aga is the focus of attention in the simple country kitchen.

The completed sofa.

A large modern sofa is essential for comfort. Make one from balsa wood and cover with fabric in a bold colour. This sofa is suitable for any modern interior.

To make a sofa

You will need:
- 2 strips of balsa, one ⅛in (3mm) thick and the other ½in (12mm) thick
- Non-fray material
- 2 small pieces of stripwood or wood moulding for the arms

All measurements are approximate – adjust for the size of sofa you want. The measurements given will provide a sofa equivalent to 6ft (180cm) in length.

Method

1 For the base, cut balsa ⅝in (16mm) deep by 3in (76mm) long.
2 For the back, cut balsa approximately 1¼in (32mm) high and 3in (76mm) long. Glue back to base (see diagram 1).
3 Cover the balsa with non-fray fabric. Cut a strip of fabric 3in (76mm) long and wide enough to wrap and glue over the base and back, with the join underneath the base.
4 Cut a paper pattern of the end of the sofa, including the back, and cut a piece of fabric to this shape for each end (see diagram 2).

Diagram 1

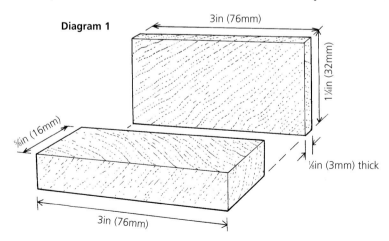

3in (76mm)

1¼in (32mm)

⅝in (16mm)

⅛in (3mm) thick

3in (76mm)

The galleried bedroom has a planked floor made from iron-on planking, finished with a semi-matt varnish. The bed is futon-style, covered with a colourful fabric spread (see page 102). The only other furniture in the low-ceilinged room is a small table and a rocking chair, which only needed a coat of varnish to finish.

Diagram 2

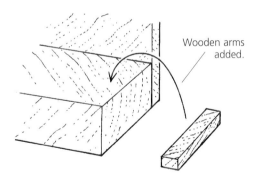

Wooden arms added.

Glue on carefully. In this scale, provided you use non-fray fabric, it will look neat.

5 Add a wooden arm at each end of the sofa, made from a piece of thin stripwood or narrow picture frame moulding. Apply general-purpose glue to the edge of the wood only. To avoid smears, leave the glue to become tacky before pressing the wooden arm into place. Leave for several hours to allow the glue to set firm.

To finish the sofa, hand sew two cushions. Use narrow ribbon or braid folded over several times. Slipstitch the edges together, leaving only one join to fold in and sew neatly. An extra scrap of ribbon pushed inside will be sufficient stuffing to make a squashy cushion.

Checklist of Tudor features

Tudor houses vary a great deal in both size and status, although they all have one thing in common – timber framing. The suggestions for decoration and furnishing in this section should help you to decide what would suit your house best, and how much to include. Here is a quick-reference list of features common to all Tudor houses:

- Timber framing,
- Plastered walls,
- Oak or stone floors,
- Inglenook fireplace with log fire,
- Painted or stencilled decoration and/or tapestries,
- Oak furniture.

10 *The English cottage*

Above **Brick infill and a shaggy thatch give this cottage a truly rural appearance.**

Cottages were built of humble materials – a surprising number of sixteenth-century English cottages still in use today have walls of wattle and daub construction – a framework made of branches lashed together, infilled with twigs and rubble and plastered over. In countryside where stone was available, cottages were roughly built from rubble stone. There are a huge number of styles to choose from, and dolls' house makers working in 1/24 seem to provide all the variations. Here are a few examples:

Devonshire stone cottage, local variation on ridging to thatch

Based on a cottage at Berry Pomeroy in Devon, this stone cottage shows a different style of thatch with a narrow ridging.

Scottish 'but and ben'

A Scottish crofter's two-room cottage, known as a 'but and ben', is neat and appealing. The black paintwork contrasts well with the traditional white rendered finish, known as 'harling'. The maker has provided a working letter flap and a rainwater downpipe.

Stone-walled cottage with thatch

Another regional variation in a beautifully detailed cottage. Stone walls with brick surrounds are peculiar to an area of Oxfordshire.

Cottage ornée

In the eighteenth century, the fashion for a weekend home began with the introduction of the cottage ornée, a vision of life in the countryside dreamed up by eccentric town dwellers. The cottage shown is based on Circular Cottage, designed by John Nash.

Cottage exterior decoration

All the cottages shown above are ready decorated, and it is obvious that the makers have enjoyed their work. To finish an undecorated cottage, stone cladding can be added (see page 51).

Hints on thatching

There are a number of different ways of reproducing thatch, and all of them are time consuming. Coconut fibre, raffia and broom bristles are all suitable materials. The chosen material should be cut into short lengths, made up into bundles 1in (25mm) wide, and carefully flattened. Everyone evolves their own method, but one which works well is to glue each bundle on to a thin strip of card or wood, ready to apply, so that it does not scatter around.

Thin staves of narrow stripwood should be glued across the roof at intervals and the bundles (known as 'yealms') should be glued on in rows, starting at the bottom of the roof, each row overlapping the one underneath in the same way as rows of slates. Note that the first row should overhang the edge of the roof.

Dormer windows and porches need to be covered separately, and it is best to do this

Thatch is a basic form of roofing that has been used in many countries. The Japanese thatched roof shown illustrates the different style in the East, with a singular form of ridge and a great deal of mossy growth. This miniature was made in Japan.

before starting on the main roof. The ridge which tops the thatch can be added in a variety of regional styles (see pages 65 and 70) and the pattern stitched using a strong needle and carpet thread.

Essentially a cottage, but with a distinctive difference, eighteenth-century toll houses have a unique charm. Round or octagonal examples, often with pretty Gothick windows, can still be found. This attractive miniature is based on one at Chew Magna, Somerset.

Cottage interior decoration

Cottage interior decoration is best kept simple – white or off-white emulsion paint looks good, and like the Tudor house, a touch of pink or ochre will give some variation. A small stencilled design can be added, perhaps used round a window or fireplace.

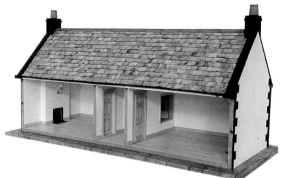

An inside view of the 'but and ben' (see page 65) The 'but' is the kitchen, kept warm by a range fitted on the end wall. The typically Scottish feature of a box bed built into the inside wall takes advantage of the warmth from the range. Planked flooring updates the original earth floor, and a tiled fireplace is fitted in the 'ben'.

Furnishing

Furniture will depend largely on whether the cottage is unaltered from earlier times or whether it is intended for modern living. Many old cottages today are used as weekend homes, and the rooms can be furnished with modern furniture and colourful textiles.

A two-room cottage which demonstrates just how small the accommodation could be for a large family, even with the weatherboarded outshot extension. The style of thatch is unusual but based on a real cottage, and must have caused problems in wet weather. The miniature cottage is fully lit.

Floors

The original floors might well have been of beaten mud, but later residents soon altered that. Most will have been replaced by quarry tiles, brick or planking.

An attractive cottage interior with pink-washed walls and a dog-leg staircase. Note the low-ceilinged bedroom; originally such a cottage would have had only a ladder up to the attic room; the staircase would be a later addition.

A cottage living room can be much more cluttered, with brass and copper ornaments and the cosy atmosphere created by a glowing fire and the lived-in look. This homely scene is set in a room box made from a kit, complete with inglenook fireplace and oak plate rack to allow for even more ornaments.

Fix any ornaments or cooking utensils down so that they do not roll away and disappear. It can be quite tricky to use a small enough piece of Blu-tack or Gripwax, so that it will not show on a shelf or table. The best method is to attach a miniscule blob to the surface first, and then place the object on top. Press into place firmly but carefully, to avoid breakages. To arrange plates on a dresser, attach the plate to the vertical surface of the wood, not to the shelf underneath, using the same method. The Blu-tack should be in the centre of the plate so that it will not stand crooked. Tweezers can be useful for putting tiny ornaments in place.

A dresser in a cottage kitchen is the ideal way to show off a selection of rustic pottery.

Cottage gardens

A neat, pretty garden surrounds this charming cottage, based on a Devon example.

The urge to surround a cottage with a garden can be almost irresistible, so much so that some sort of garden is almost an integral part of the dolls' house cottage rather than a separate entity. A token garden can be achieved by attaching climbing plants and a small border to the walls (see page 18).

If you plan a small garden around the cottage, one easy method of deciding how much you can fit into it is to make a few card frames (draw round picture frames or books as a guide) and try them round the cottage. It is much easier to work out what you can fit into a given space if you can see a mock-up in front of you rather than a scaled-down plan on paper.

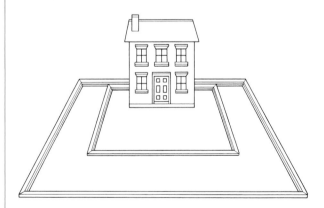

Use picture frames to check out a suitable size for a cottage garden.

11 *Decorating a Georgian house*

This classical Georgian house is supplied undecorated. There are six well-proportioned rooms, a hall, staircase and two landings.

facade and well-proportioned rooms is an equally interesting decorative project.

Exterior decoration

Stone-coloured paint is effective on a classical facade. There are a whole range of stone colours, from cool to warm, so even with the basic

The perfect proportions of classical Georgian houses look as good in a small scale as they do in reality, and for the collector, this is the perfect showcase for miniature furniture. The style appeals to many talented professional miniaturists, so there is a good choice of beautifully finished pieces to fill the rooms.

Classical Georgian houses are based on the Palladian style taken up with enthusiasm by those rich enough to build new and impressive homes in the eighteenth century. In complete contrast to the Tudor buildings featured earlier in the book, a Georgian house, with its plain

The facade of this house is based on the architecture of Palladio, and following Italian precedent, would be built of stone. In 1/24, paint is the best option.

decision made, there is an element of choice. It can be helpful to make a shade card to try out sample colours which will be next to each other on the house, to see how they will look together.

Do not forget that colours may look a little different on wood. As well as keeping the sample card for reference, try out the shade on a spare piece of wood before making your final choice.

The colours chosen for this house are all in semi-matt finish, the main colours are regular decorator's paint.

Main facade	York stone – a pale stone shade
Architectural detailing	Georgian stone – a warmer shade to emphasize the detail
Roof	Two coats of mid-stone model enamel which has a greenish hue, plus one coat of semi-matt varnish
Window frames	Georgian white – an off-white with a creamy tone
Front door	Dark green model enamel
Chimney pots	Terracotta – a mix of stone plus a dash of raw sienna gouache

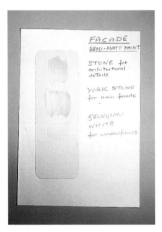

Plan colour schemes and make shade cards as tests and to keep for reference.

Before painting the exterior, remove the front door and put hinges and screws in a container with a secure lid (a plastic film container is ideal). Also remove the fastening hook and screws and keep them safe to put back on after decoration is completed.

The front opening of a dolls' house is often a very neat fit, and a layer of paint on the edges may make it too tight to close properly. Check after undercoating and if necessary, sand off a little from these edges – wrap the glasspaper round a block of wood to make

sure you keep the edges straight. Apply only one top coat of paint.

Roof and chimneys

Paint the chimneys first, wipe off any drips of paint and allow to dry thoroughly before starting on the roof. When painting a sloping roof, check immediately after painting and again a few minutes later, to make sure there are no paint runs to spoil the surface.

A lift-off roof can be placed on wooden supports for painting; this will allow the lower edges to dry cleanly.

Window frames

Some houses are supplied with plastic window frames which do not need painting. Most period-style houses have wooden frames, and of these, sash windows are particularly tedious to paint because of the many sections.

Whatever type of window frame you are painting, sand gently first to make sure the wood is smooth – an emery board (designed for nail care) is ideal for this purpose. Use emulsion paint instead of regular undercoat – this will avoid a thick build up of paint. Sand again and apply top coat.

This house has eight (non-opening) 'sash' windows, making a total of seventy-eight individual panes. A perfect finish can be achieved with care and patience.

When painting sash windows, follow the same sequence with each window to avoid missing out any parts of the glazing bars – undersides, sides and then top and bottom of each. Don't neglect the inside. You will fit the glazing against the bars inside so it is important that they are really smooth.

> Sanding will generate a fine dust which needs to be removed before each coat of paint. A suction cleaner is the most effective way to deal with dust.

Front door

Paint the front door in your chosen colour. Undercoat is unnecessary if you use model enamel. Paint one side of the door, the side and top edges and leave to dry laid on a small piece of wood before painting the second side. Do not paint the bottom edge or the door may not fit over the step or floor. Add any door furniture and refit the hinges.

Georgian interior decoration

A classical house can conform to conventional decorative schemes and look stunning. Authentic eighteenth-century paint colours, wallpapers with a dash of Chinoiserie, paintings

A variety of ideas for each room. When open, the house will be seen as a whole, so it is important that decorative schemes look good when seen together.

and sculpture and a formal arrangement of furniture all set the style. Stone or marble fireplaces (mimicked in cast resin) and decorative cornices will enhance the rooms.

Try some colour co-ordination with samples of paper and flooring materials and sort out some pictures to use for trompe l'oeil effects. Plan the decorations so that adjacent rooms do not have clashing colours. Before wallpapering, remove any fastening hooks inside and mark the holes with a pin or small tack for easy relocation.

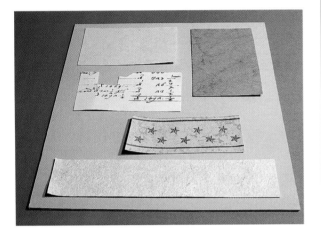

More ideas using colour and texture.

Entrance hall and staircase

The entrance hall and staircase can be impressive; they are your first view when you enter a real house, and set the standard for what is to follow.

Painting a staircase

Most staircases can be removed for decoration. If however the staircase is fixed in, it can be difficult to see properly when painting balusters. Prop up a piece of white card behind the stairs if you are using dark-coloured paint, or black card if you have selected a pale shade, so that the detail stands out. Do not attempt to paint parts

which cannot be seen. In their enthusiasm to get it right, new hobbyists sometimes try to do this – but resist the temptation, as it really is unnecessary. When you add furniture do not fix a mirror on a wall where it will reflect the unpainted section.

The grand effect of the staircase is emphasized by the addition of green and gold ribbon used as carpet. Small prints of 'painted' scenes over the doorways provide additional decoration on the delicately coloured 'plastered' walls.

Georgian paintwork was often in rich, warm colours such as deep red, brown or green. Rooms in 1/24 will often look small and cramped if the paintwork is too dark, but the staircase is a good place to use an authentic shade. The balusters and handrail in this house are painted in bronze-green model enamel, which shows up well against the pale walls. The sides of the stair treads are painted to resemble stone.

Trompe l'oeil effects

Trompe l'oeil works especially well in 1/24. A painting with a classical subject will suit a Georgian house, and if it covers a whole wall (see below) it need not be framed. Place it immediately below the cornice and above a dado rail, which will form convenient borders.

Door frames

In a formal, classical house, an appropriate door frame is essential if the interior is to look finished, whether or not there is an actual door in place. Cut two pieces of stripwood or moulding the height of the doorway and one piece to fit over the top. Mitre the joins at the outer top edges of the doorway, to give a neat finish.

The painting on the landing wall is a reproduction of a genuine trompe l'oeil painting by the late Rex Whistler, which is in the dining room of Plas Newydd on the Isle of Anglesey. Used at the back of the stairs, it appears truly three-dimensional.

Doors and doorways

Most dolls' houses have simple openings for internal doorways. Occasionally doors are ready fitted or can be purchased separately. If you do not propose to fit internal doors, paint the edges of the aperture with white semi-matt paint before wallpapering or painting walls.

Fitting an internal door yourself in this size may cause problems because of the exceptionally small size of hinges and screws, if they are to scale. Use impact glue to fix hinges on to the door and the inside of the door frame, and pin on with brass pins rather than screws.

A door frame should be fitted after the walls have been painted or papered. The doorways are close to the front edge in this house. The stripwood used for the sides of the door frame exactly fills the gap between the doorway and the front of the house. This gap can be awkward to fill in any other way, as skirting board of such a short length can appear clumsy.

Using a mitre box and saw

To cut the mitre for the joins in a door frame you will need to use a miniature metal mitre box and saw (available from hobby shops). Several makes are available, for example X-Acto mitre box no.7533 and knife handle no.5 fitted with saw blade no.239. It is important to use the correct size of blade to fit the mitre box you have chosen, to avoid wear. Replacement blades are available.

A mitre box and saw is not included in the list of essential tools (see page 26) as it will only be needed when making door frames, window frames or fireplaces, or fitting skirting boards or cornice, which will not be necessary with all house styles. But if you do have one, it is a useful tool for making mini picture frames.

Diagram 1   Cutting the mitred corners for a fireplace, window frame or door frame

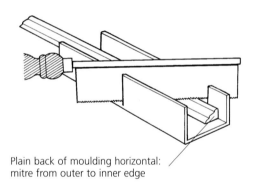

Plain back of moulding horizontal: mitre from outer to inner edge

Fitting a door frame

The style of door frame shown (see page 75) is based on many in Italian villas – a piece of plain stripwood on either side, as above, but without the mitred join at the top, where a piece of heavier moulding is added straight across to form an impressive pediment. The top of the moulding fits flush with the front but the inner edge is cut at an angle to show off the detailed moulding. This idea can also be used to emphasize a doorway in the middle

Diagram 2   Mitre-cut moulding on a door pediment

Diagram 3   The correct angle

Plain back of moulding upright

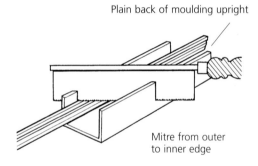

Mitre from outer to inner edge

of a wall, in this case both ends of the top moulding should be angled (see diagram 2).

When cutting the ends of the moulding to use over a doorway in this way, the wood should be placed in the mitre box with the plain back of the moulding upright (see diagram 3).

Internal window frames

Window frames can be glued in place after painting or papering internal walls. One simple idea is to glue on narrow braid; it is neat, will look attractive, and is a good option if you do not want to have curtained windows. For a more realistic look, make wooden window frames. Alternatively, added curtains

or blinds will cover the top and side edges of the window and a thin strip of wood, glued on as a windowsill, will be all that is necessary.

Fitting skirting board and cornice

Georgian houses need the formality of skirting boards and cornice to look their best. The simplest method is to use plain stripwood and butt the ends together in the corners.

Diagram 4   The correct angle for cutting mitred corners in wood moulding for skirting boards.

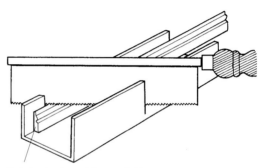

Plain back of moulding upright

Diagram 5

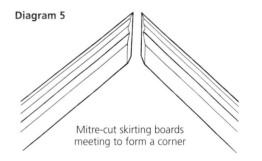

Mitre-cut skirting boards meeting to form a corner

As a decorative, unified effect, the inside front of the house is papered with giftwrap which reproduces an old manuscript. Curtains or braid would detract from this; instead, wooden window frames with mitred corners are fitted (see diagram 1 on page 76). The lower window frame has not yet been fitted over the papered front; compare the completed effect on the other windows. The front door is likely to have heavy use, so the hinges supplied by the dolls' house maker are not to scale.

Always check before fixing any added frame or curtain that it will not brush against the front edge of the floors inside the house and prevent the front closing. If this is the case, a paper border, which is thinner than braid or wood, is the only option. Cut and fix a length from wallpaper border in an appropriate colour or design.

Reproduction 1/24 wooden period mouldings are superior and will give an authentic effect. To fit these, mitred corners are again essential so that the grooves in the mouldings fit together neatly (see pages 78 and 79).

Place the moulding in the mitre box with the plain back upright and cut from the outer to the inner edge. Cutting mitre joints can be confusing for the beginner; follow the instructions (see diagrams) and double-check the angle of cut before you start. Look at a real example in your own home to see how skirting board fits together in the corner of a room (see diagram 5).

In 1/24, any gap at a join, however tiny, will show up badly. It is essential to fill the joins between mitred corners of stripwood after fitting, because even if they fit perfectly, the join line will be noticeable. A little interior filler can be wiped over the join, using a wooden cocktail stick, and sanded gently when dry, then painted over.

Room arrangements

The principal rooms in this house are formal and impressive, just as they would have been in the eighteenth century. The salon and dining room are on the first floor, with a bedroom and study/library above, while there are two kitchens below in contrasting styles. English and Italian influences are combined to make an attractive and pleasing interior with a few surprises.

The salon

Chinese-style wallpaper is appropriate for an eighteenth-century room and can be simulated in card. Postcard-size designs are often the

The salon is much too grand to be termed a sitting room. The decorations and furniture are elegant and delicate. The spinet, with its charming floral decoration, is a reminder that long before the advent of television, music was a regular after-dinner entertainment.

The dining room is simply and beautifully furnished with 'antique' oak furniture. Like the salon, the ceiling is painted in a pale pink-tinged white enlivened by a gilded centrepiece to add an air of grandeur and formality.

correct scale to suit 1/24, and although it is a little more trouble to glue on separate cards rather than one sheet of wallpaper, the effect works well. Remember to use general-purpose glue to make sure that the cards do not curl up at the corners.

Below the dado rail, a pink-tinged rough-textured paper is used to reproduce a plaster effect, so that the room is not swamped with pattern (see also the dining room).

The dining room

Like the other formal rooms, the dining room is floored with 'marble', an idea copied from Palladian villas in Italy. With the exception of the ground floor, this would be unacceptable in reality owing to the weight, but is fine in a dolls' house. The floors are of marble-patterned card – the colours are subtle and the size of the marbling is in the right scale, which is important to give a realistic effect (see page 31).

The bedroom

Dolls' house bedrooms are not usually large enough for a great deal of furniture once the centrepiece, the bed, is in place. Pretty decorations are important and can be more feminine and frivolous than in other rooms. First decide on a colour scheme and then search out accessories which will emphasize and accent it, for example, a painting to hang on the wall in the right colouring can add to the effect.

The starting point for the pretty colour scheme in the Georgian bedroom is a patterned floor, simulating a hand-painted design, with blue-green as the dominant colour – a new use for an unusual greeting card. The exquisite painted chest adds emphasis. Although there is little furniture, all the essentials are there.

The border round the room is made of thin silk braided roses, which is also used as tiebacks for the knitted lace bed hangings. Golden stars are cut and fitted in a random arrangement over the ceiling and there is a small shower of stars on the wall behind the bed.

The library/study

It always enhances an otherwise conventional interior to include an unusual room which will develop an idea which appeals to you. It can be designed to suit a particular story line. As an example, this library/study is tailored to fit the personality of the imagined patrician owner.

Naturally, there should be plenty of books in such a room. Remember when making books to suit this scale that you will need to reduce the number of pages as well as the page size, as the finished book will look clumsy otherwise. The fake bookcase towards the back of the room is a magazine cutting. Look through old magazines until you find a pictured example which is of a

Left The centre-piece of the marble floor is a reproduction of a classical painting, which is echoed on the ceiling above. The paintings on the walls reinforce the Italianate feeling. The pyramid mineral sample is introduced as an object for scientific study, and is independent of dolls' house scale.

The completed trompe l'oeil 'bookcase'.

suitable size and clearly printed. Glue to the wall and fit a wooden surround of thin stripwood to give the 'bookcase' some depth. Library steps and a few real books in front will add to the realistic effect.

Sculpture

Sculpture is almost obligatory in a grand house, whether it is of plaster or bronze (see page 16). To provide a realistic bronze classical bust, repaint an inexpensive pewter miniature with a metallic finish.

1 Paint with one coat of dark brown model enamel. This will dry very quickly on metal or resin.

2 Top coat with bronze metallic model enamel, rubbing off here and there with tissue or rag before it dries to reveal the duller brown.

The repainted bust is now a convincing replica of a bronze casting.

You can use this technique for other settings too – try a greenish-brown model enamel and a gold top coat for a convincing effect on an Art Nouveau or Art Deco statuette.

The kitchen gains an added dimension from the fake doorway at the back of the room. This bit of trompe l'oeil is part of a greeting card, showing a drawing done by John Ruskin during a visit to Italy.

An updated kitchen

A modern kitchen is another surprise in this setting, updating the house for an owner who may have inherited the antique furniture featured in other rooms.

This is an up-market kitchen and an Aga is essential. In a 1/12 kitchen it is usual to set an Aga or a range into a recess, but in 1/24 a tiled panel works well and creates much the same effect without taking up valuable space. Surround the panel with a frame made from three thin pieces of stripwood to provide a neat edge. (Mitre the corners in the same way as for a picture frame, see page 76).

The replica tiling is extended to form a hearth under and in front of the Aga.

The right type of food is tremendously important in a kitchen. The examples displayed here were professionally made and include some extremely realistic salami, especially to suit the English/Italian theme. Fruit, such as apples and oranges, is the easiest to model yourself, with one of the modelling clays which can then be painted.

The original, much older kitchen, has been retained in this house to provide a contrast in styles and is mainly Victorian (see page 40).

Decorative ideas

The decoration of this house is partly standard Georgian and partly idiosyncratic. Although the main reception rooms are typically Georgian, other rooms show a strong Italian classical influence with the use of fake marble and 'fresco' paintings. These ideas were taken up by many English gentlemen in the eighteenth century, on their return from the grand tour.

None of the schemes given are intended to be followed exactly, but will, I hope, be a starting-point to adapt for further ideas to use in your own dolls' house.

12 *Decorating a Georgian town house*

A splendid dolls' house which shows Georgian brickwork at its best. It is based on a real house which was refaced in the eighteenth century and the miniaturist has included the unusual original feature of a sundial on the facade, with an inscription to Robert Adam, who no doubt inspired the builder. The bricks were made and painted by the dolls' house maker. The detail achieved in 1/24 is astounding.

Georgian town houses were frequently built in brick, and many older houses were refronted in brick during the eighteenth century to give a more modern appearance. Georgian brickwork is a delight, and the dolls' house enthusiast with a plain house to complete has a number of options for producing a brick facade.

Brick cladding

Bricks (and roof tiles) in one piece

The easiest method is to cut and glue on Georgian-style brick cladding supplied in a sheet. Such cladding is realistic, a far cry from the 'brick paper' sometimes used on Victorian dolls' houses, which tore easily and soon looked shabby. Roofing tiles are another option supplied in sheet form to complete the exterior.

Plasticized cladding in sheet form makes reproducing Georgian brickwork easy for the hobbyist. This sheet includes a section of brick arranged in a herringbone pattern, which can be used to line a fireplace recess (see page 89) or as a garden path.

Real brick and slate

Another, more time-consuming method is to use real brick slips and roof tiles (see the Tudor example on page 49). Roof tiles and slates are available in a variety of colours so that you can choose a regional variation to suit the imagined site of your house.

For the more confident hobbyist, brick slips and real slates will be realistic.

Weatherboard (siding)

Wood siding immediately brings Shaker houses to mind, as well as modern homes in many parts of the United States. However, weatherboarding has been a feature of houses in some parts of England since the eighteenth century. There are also Georgian houses

Slates are available in a range of colours based on regional variations.

finished in this way in parts of London (Hampstead, for example). Like brick facing, siding can be added either in individual lengths or in one piece; either looks realistic. Sheet siding in simulated wood is ready coloured, whereas real wood can be painted or stained as you wish.

The town house interior

The interior of a Georgian town house can be simple or grand, according to taste and to suit the exterior. For the traditional English look, the walls can be painted with Adam green or blue emulsion. Pearl (a lovely pale shade of green) which is now available in historic colour paint ranges, was also much favoured for the best rooms. Off-white semi-matt paintwork is also appropriate.

Ceiling decoration

Plaster roundels and painted centrepieces were a feature of the better-class Georgian town house. Painted decoration is easily reproduced by gluing on an appropriate pictured painting (see page 80) and you can provide a good facsimile of elaborate plasterwork without too much effort.

Sections of doyleys cut to illustrate possible designs which could be used as ceiling centre-pieces. White paper doyleys can be painted over to match the ceiling colour. Occasionally, gold or silver can look impressive in a grand room, but cannot be painted over successfully.

Use a doyley

Paper doyleys in cutwork designs and a range of sizes are available from good stationers and can be used to create any size of ceiling design from a small central medallion to all over coverage. Paper gives a raised effect which is exactly right in this scale.

Method

1 Measure the size of the ceiling and decide on the best size for the centrepiece.
2 Carefully cut out the central part of the design to suit, using sharp scissors.
3 Apply one coat of emulsion to the ceiling and, when the paint is dry, mark the centrepoint.
4 Glue on the doyley design, matching the centrepoints, using general-purpose adhesive. Press on carefully but firmly to avoid tears in the delicate paper.
5 Apply a second coat of emulsion over the whole doyley and ceiling.

Fixtures and fittings

Chimneypiece is the original term for a fireplace surround, which we now refer to simply as a fireplace. In the early eighteenth century, fireplaces were plain and simple, without even a mantelshelf above, and were usually painted to match any surrounding wooden panelling.

Make a chimney breast

A chimney breast can be made from a ¼in (6mm) thick piece of balsa wood, long enough to reach from the floor to the ceiling. Mark the centre, measure carefully and cut out a rectangle for the grate aperture.

In a 1/24 room it will save space if you dispense with a chimney breast and fit the fireplace flush to the wall.

Make a plain fireplace

To make a plain fireplace, all you need is three pieces of thin stripwood to outline the space for the grate, which can be backed with black card (see diagram 1). There is no need to mitre the corners, as this was a later refinement.

A further addition dating from slightly later in the Georgian period, is to add a piece of thin picture frame moulding to the inner edge of the plain stripwood. Here, the corners can be mitred (see diagram 2).

Diagram 1 Plain early Georgian fireplace

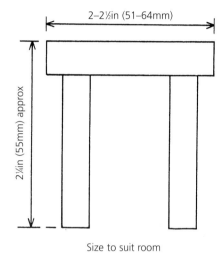

2–2½in (51–64mm)

2¼in (55mm) approx

Size to suit room

However, it is useful to have a mantelshelf to display ornaments or candlesticks (see page 80). Here is a design for a fireplace with a little more detail from the mid-eighteenth century.

Diagram 2 Mid-eighteenth century

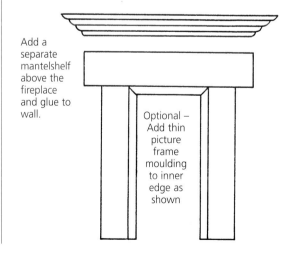

Add a separate mantelshelf above the fireplace and glue to wall.

Optional – Add thin picture frame moulding to inner edge as shown

A separate mantelshelf is fitted above the fireplace, a common arrangement at this time. The outer corners of the mantelshelf should be cut at an angle in the same way as the pediment over a door frame (see page 76). In 1/12 scale it would be necessary to add a side section to fill the gap, but in 1/24 this is not needed as the gap is so tiny.

A typical height for a 1/24 Georgian fireplace including mantelshelf is 2⅛in (55mm). Width varies from 2in (51mm) to 2½in (64mm) to suit the chosen style and the size of the room.

During the latter part of the Georgian period, fireplaces became very elaborate and were made of marble, or of wood with added mouldings of 'composition', painted to simulate marble. A decorative fireplace in cast resin, similar to those used in the Georgian house featured on pages 76–81 will also suit the grander town house.

Floors

Stone, rather than marble floors were usual on the ground floor, and card offers a simple way to provide these (fit as you would a marble floor, see page 31). For the Georgian house, try to find pictured flagstones or a better class of stone than that used in a Tudor house (compare page 54).

Iron-on floorboards in oak, pine or mahogany are also suitable. To fit see page 31. Georgian floorboards were left unpolished, but a coat of matt varnish will give a good finish without being too shiny.

Another authentic finish for unpolished floorboards in a Georgian house is to wash over with a coat of pale grey emulsion paint.

Mix a very little grey model enamel with some white emulsion and thin with water to make a wash. Rub over the floorboards with a rag rather than a brush, and rub off most of the paint with a dry rag. Georgian floorboards were kept clean by sprinkling them with sand and sweeping daily, which gave a greyish tint to the wood.

Furniture

The furnishings described in the more conventional rooms of the Georgian house will also be suitable for a town house.

Here is a quick check list of Georgian interior features for reference:

- Cornice and skirting board, optional dado rail,
- Ceiling roundel or painted centrepiece,
- Unpolished, wooden planked floors; simulated marble or stone,
- Fireplace **early Georgian** can be plain and of wood, **late Georgian** were of marble and much more elaborate (1/24 miniature versions are available in cast resin),
- Chinese-style wallpaper,
- Door frames, sometimes surmounted by a pediment.

In full size, minuscule variations in the carving on a set of chairs will not be noticeable, but a 1/24 set, where any difference would immediately stand out, is a challenge for the miniaturist.

13 *Victorian and Edwardian style*

The large Victorian house

Based on a house built in the Georgian style in the early part of Queen Victoria's reign, this miniature was commissioned as a replica of the owner's home, a former vicarage. Even in 1/24, it is approximately 28in (710mm) square and has twelve rooms plus the conservatory. It is fully lit.

Victorian country gentlemen enjoyed incorporating elements from earlier periods in their sometimes vast houses. Victorian and Edwardian interiors are great fun to decorate and furnish, and it is worth considering this style if you plan a large house. One with many rooms would be a never-ending source of pleasure to fill, either for the collector or in order to make many of the contents yourself.

Such a house could be furnished as though additions had been made over generations, in an easy, comfortable style which would happily include a mixture of periods to show the passage of time.

A large house offers further pleasure for the miniaturist in arranging the servants' quarters in a different way from the family rooms, with simple furniture and uncovered wooden floors. The conservatory can be filled with flowers and fruit, and garden furniture too, with perhaps a table set out with appetizing food and a tea service all ready for afternoon tea, just as it would have been in the house's heyday.

The smaller home

On a more homely scale, a small villa with perhaps four rooms might be a more manageable project. The late Victorian and Edwardian periods provide the first opportunity to include a bathroom in a period dolls' house, and a miniature suite of fittings based on original designs will be an attractive addition.

Bathrooms were a novelty and not nearly as comfortable as they are today; floors were of linoleum and there was no central heating. However the bathroom can be made to look attractive with tiled walls and the addition of a potted plant. A clawfoot bathtub or even a hip bath would be suitable, as well as the newly invented flushing water closet.

Whatever the size of the house, the kitchen was the hub of the Victorian home. Brick or stone floors were usual as often the kitchen was in a basement. Pottery and porcelain in 1/24 are plentiful and even the smallest kitchen gadgets are reproduced in pewter, which can be painted, or in etched nickel silver.

A grey stone villa with red roof tiles and bright paintwork. Victorian house exteriors were more colourful than in previous eras. Stained glass was also incorporated where possible, and the miniaturists have provided a window in the side wall over the staircase.

A range will be the centrepiece of the kitchen, whether with glowing coals if the house is electrified, or painted in simulation; the other essential is a dresser filled with a matching set of plates or a variety of pottery. Add food to taste!

The mangle and sink in this spick-and-span kitchen are evidence of the weekly wash, which was generally done in an adjacent scullery or even outside in the yard. (The realistic mangle included here is a fridge magnet.) The grandfather clock in the corner and a tobacco jar on the mantelpiece are as authentic as the mouse on the floor.

A range is essential in a Victorian kitchen. This model is an inexpensive fridge magnet and the perfect size to suit 1/24. It is complete with glowing coals and cooking pans, and the ash tray pulls out.

14 *Shops*

A shop is an attractive alternative to a fully-furnished home for many miniaturists, and is the ideal display unit to show off a specialized collection, whether it is of furniture, food or pottery. Miniature clothing and hats will also look their best in a showroom setting, where they can be laid out to advantage.

A tea shop

Another idea is to use a small shop as a tea room. The one shown is fitted out in 1930s style, based on many real examples in Shakespeare country, where some things have changed little since then.

The ground floor, which leads straight off the street without any entrance hall, is used as the tea room, so there is plenty of delicious looking food. In this type of establishment, cakes are often for sale to take away as well as to eat on the premises.

Complete the 1930s effect with curtains hung from a wooden pole by means of brass rings. Use a cocktail stick and brass jump rings

Above **A row of one-room shops, each measuring 6in (152mm) in all directions, is a real possibility in 1/24 without taking up too much space. The shops can be added one at a time and offer the hobbyist a ready excuse to try out display skills. For anyone who enjoys making or collecting many tiny items, a shop is the best possible choice.**

Below **Morning coffee and afternoon tea are the busiest times in this establishment. The astonishingly detailed food was professionally made, and to emphasize the idea that it was cooked on the premises, a 1930s gas stove can be glimpsed in the kitchen leading off the tea room.**

Patterned curtains give a 1930s look to the bay window of the tea shop.

(from a craft shop). Attach the pole to the house wall with small brass picture hooks – but first check that the screws are shorter than the thickness of the wall, otherwise they might go right through and damage the house front. Glue small wooden beads at each end of the pole to represent finials.

Above **An antique-look shop made in reclaimed pine and complete with brass lock and key, is the perfect unit for the collector who does not wish to decorate.**

Building shops from plans

Building a shop (or shops) from plans is an option for the hobbyist with woodworking skills. Plans for the ones shown include drawings, detailed instructions and a list of the tools and materials needed. Door and window packs can be bought separately. Dormer windows are an optional extra.

Decoration is a matter of personal choice, and the finished building can be adapted to use either as two shops, side by side as shown, or if one large establishment is preferred, an extra window could be fitted instead of one of the pair of front doors.

Below **A pair of shops built from a set of plans. The roof is covered with tile sheeting. The windows and doors are of white plastic, which can be painted if a colour is preferred.**

15 *Twentieth-century room boxes*

Twentieth-century house design began with Charles Rennie Mackintosh, the innovator. In his own lifetime, his work was more appreciated on the Continent than in his native Scotland, but his ideas continue to influence modern architects to this day. His austere style has now become so popular in real life that many miniaturists are drawn to recreate rooms which include Mackintosh decorations and furniture.

Mackintosh enjoyed the contrast of a very dark room next to one which was almost entirely white, to offer a change of mood. His

An evocative 'lounge' from the 1930s–40s, arranged in a room box made from a kit which includes the then fashionable 'brick' fireplace. The essential three-piece suite of that era is available separately.

own dining room was papered with a grey-brown wrapping paper and then stencilled with a rose motif on lattice panels, almost like an indoor garden – but a rather sombre one.

It is also interesting to create a room showing his influence without it being an exact reproduction of one particular room (see page 94).

Miniaturists could take a hint from Mackintosh's real life use of wrapping paper as wallpaper (see also page 29). Stencilling appears in nearly all of his houses on both walls and furniture. The makers of this setting have provided exact copies of his Dove chairs and dining table as used in the Argyle Street tea rooms. The large piece at the back of the room is a Smoker's Cabinet.

Room boxes

Most of the single rooms featured in this section have been designed and completed as individual settings in open-fronted room boxes made from foamboard. These settings demonstrate that it is possible to achieve a professional finish by using inexpensive and recycled materials which are a little different from the standard ranges of wallpaper and flooring made specifically for the scale.

Such rooms are straightforward to complete; wall coverings and floorings can be glued in place or attached with double-sided adhesive tape (see page 94 and page 103). They range from a Mackintosh room through the styles of decoration of the 1920s and 30s and lastly, the epitome of aspirational present-day living, a loft. In most cases, inexpensive furniture is modified or transformed with paint and full instructions for achieving these effects are given and illustrated. In some settings, professionally made miniatures are featured which will appeal to the collector (see Art Deco on page 98).

The section ends with two versions of a vignette – an even smaller setting which can be personalized as an enchanting gift to a friend or relative.

Make your own room box

It is easy to make a simple three-sided room box from foamboard to try out initial ideas, and then transfer the contents to a more permanent, wooden structure. Most of the boxes featured were made open ended, in order to give the camera a better view – I added the end wall after the photographs were taken.

To make a room box that is suitable for experimental settings, use 3.5 mm (approx ³⁄₁₆in) foamboard, which is easy to cut with a craft knife and raised-edge metal ruler (see tools on page 26).

Method

1 Cut walls and floor, using the lines on a cutting mat as a guide to make sure that the edges are straight and the corners square. A ceiling is optional and can be added later. The front can be left open (see diagram).

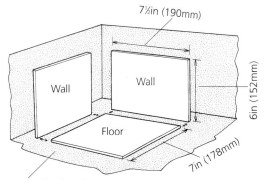

7½in (190mm)

Wall

Wall

6in (152mm)

Floor

7in (178mm)

Use part of a shoe box as a temporary support

2 Cut off part of a thick cardboard shoe box (see diagram). This will provide temporary support while glue sets – very thin cardboard will not provide sufficient support as it may warp out of true.
3 Glue the foamboard walls together and on to the base. Place the box structure inside the shoe box shell and tape at the back with masking tape.
4 After the glue has set firmly, remove the shoe box support.

A Mackintosh room setting

Set the scene in an almost-white room by using postcards to make a distinctive wall covering. Black lines on the walls are complemented by the chairs and tables, and Mackintosh's rose 'signature' – in this case, two flowers in simple glass vases. The contrasts of black and white, light and shade, are restful. The floor panel is a flight of fancy, a beaten metal design, again taken from a greetings card. The main floor covering is a shimmering multi-coloured paper in pale pinks, green and white.

There are so many postcard and greetings card reproductions of Mackintosh designs and those by his wife, Margaret, that any number of similar schemes could be devised to include different elements of his style. Pink and purple were other colours which he favoured to use as accents.

The only colour accents in this room are the green on the walls, the pink of the roses, and the gleam of the beaten metal floor.

To provide a plain modern glass vase, use the plastic tubing which protects the end of an artist's paintbrush when bought. Cut shorter, if necessary, with sharp scissors or a craft knife. Fix on a table with a dot of Blu-tack.

The Mackintosh influence

Modernism

An all-white room has been tried from time to time by modern designers, but has never become generally popular, as most people enjoy having their favourite things scattered around and a degree of clutter. A miniature all-white room is an excellent alternative, and incredibly restful to gaze at after a hard day.

To create a modernist room, start with a floor of foamboard; the shiny surface is perfect to simulate a polished, modern flooring material. For the walls, white card covered with translucent white paper will create a light and airy effect.

Furniture should be minimal – small Perspex boxes make excellent tables. All that is needed to complete such a room is a couple of modern paintings – choose your own from a magazine or art gallery catalogue. They will look best unframed, glued on to thin white card as a mount and attached to the wall with Blu-tack or Gripwax.

In an almost all-white room, one or two colour accents make a considerable impact. The black glass bottle is Tudor in style, here transformed into an art object.

Skirting boards are unnecessary in many modern settings. They make a period room look finished but in some houses today the wall is recessed at the base to avoid kick marks. In 1/24 scale, such a small indentation would be hardly noticeable and may be omitted.

To make a floor-standing vase to hold some branches in the approved modern manner, use plastic tubing (as for the small vase in the Mackintosh room). The base can be made from a small gilt tube bead (available from a craft shops). The thin branches are taken from an artificial plant.

The Swedish room

Almost contemporary with Mackintosh, Swedish style first became accepted through the work of the artists Carl and Karin Larsson in the early 1900s. They, too, were innovators, trying out colour effects on their often home-made furniture, and they were quite prepared to repaint period furniture in bright colours.

Swedish-style decoration and furnishings have become an accepted part of modern living, and the Larssons' influence has filtered through to become an international style. Modern furnishing stores such as Habitat and IKEA stock many designs that the Larssons would recognize.

The walls of a modern Swedish room can be painted a strong pink or green. Planked floors are usually a cool blue-grey (see page 86). You can use almost any simple modern-looking furniture, painted white, with perhaps one or two pieces in bright blue or pink. Make cushions from blue and white checked ribbon, and use ribbon with a flowered trim to make borders on walls. The dining table should be covered with an embroidered cloth; the one shown in the picture is cut from an old handkerchief.

Painted furniture, well-placed flowers and a blue and white rug encapsulate the Swedish style.

The essence of Swedish style is colour and light. The basis for this look is brightly painted or white furniture, blue and white fabrics in fine stripes or small checks, and plenty of flowers. The final touch is to add blue and white striped floor rugs – those shown here are of cotton, the fringed edges made by carefully pulling out threads to the desired length.

Make a fake window

A good-sized window is essential. In a room box, a fake window works well (see picture on page 95). Reproduce lattice with nylon mesh, glued on to a piece of blue-green paper to give the effect of cool, northern light. To avoid smears use a wooden orange stick to apply the minimum amount of general-purpose glue around the edge of the card only, and leave it to become tacky before pressing into place.

Add flowering plants

Flowers and plants are always included in a Swedish room, and a row of potted plants on the windowsill will add further colour. Packs of ivy, made from brass, which are ready for painting, are inexpensive and available in most dolls' house shops. The leafy stems are flexible so that the ivy can be bent into realistic curves to trail around a window.

The stove

A huge tiled stove was the dominant feature in any Scandinavian room from the eighteenth century to the early 1900s. Such a stove will be beautifully decorated, and can be either cylindrical or square. A bought stove can be painted white and gilded, using a gold writing pen (see picture on page 95), or you can make your own square or rectangular version.

The stove is based on one in the home of Swedish artist/designers Carl and Karin Larsson. The tiles are not the more usual blue and white, but a colourful flowered design.

Make a stove

To make a stove similar to the one shown here, you need two blocks of wood to form the upper and lower parts. The height of each piece of wood is not crucial, as either the lower or upper part of the stove can be the taller, but the completed stove should reach the ceiling of the room. You will also need some pictured tiling – mine came from a greetings card showing period tiles.

Method

1 Glue the two pieces of wood together.
2 Measure and cut the card to the same height as each block of wood and wide enough to fold round the sides. Glue in place and trim to fit. Glue another piece of 'tiling' across the top of the lower part of the stove to form a shelf.
3 To make the doors, cut a rectangle of card, size approximately ¾in (19mm) wide x ½in (13mm) deep and paint with Metalcote 'burnished steel' model enamel. When dry, rub with a cloth to bring up the shine. Glue in place (see diagram for position).

Make a Swedish stove

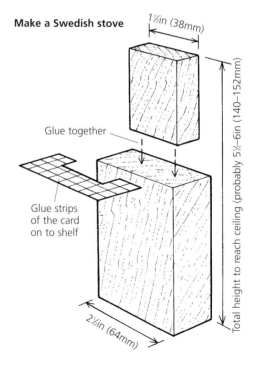

1½in (38mm)

Glue together

Glue strips of the card on to shelf

2½in (64mm)

Total height to reach ceiling (probably 5½–6in (140–152mm))

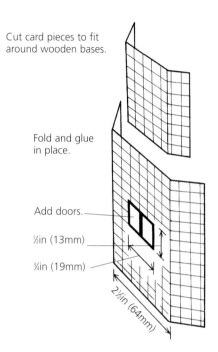

Cut card pieces to fit around wooden bases.

Fold and glue in place.

Add doors.

½in (13mm)

¾in (19mm)

2½in (64mm)

The starting point for this room is the purple and gold wallpaper, found in an exhibition catalogue. It makes a splendid background for the pair of black and gold panels, made from museum postcards. An essential element in this room style is a large oriental vase, or preferably a pair. Vases in 1/12 scale can be used as floor-standing ornaments.

If you prefer to fix miniature ceramic tiles on to the stove individually, you will need to work out the measurements accurately and cut the wood so that the tiles will fit the height and width of the two sections and also the depth of the shelf formed above the lower part.

1920s Oriental room

Oriental furniture and ornaments intrigue Europeans and Americans alike. This was particularly so in the 1920s, when some bizarre schemes were created by those rich enough to indulge their whims. Rooms were decorated in deep, rich colours, lighting was subdued, and frequently both Chinese and Japanese art treasures were included. I am sure that their owners enjoyed these exotic rooms a great deal, and it is just as much fun to make a miniature version.

Adapt a table

Imported oriental-style tables in 1/12 are widely available and can be adapted to suit 1/24.

Method

1 Strip off the varnish. Use a proprietary paint stripper, wear rubber gloves and follow the instructions on the can. Protect the work surface with layers of newspaper.
2 Sand smooth with fine glasspaper and wipe over with white spirit (mineral spirits) to provide a clean surface for repainting.
3 Cut off the curving feet, then cut the legs down to about half length. (It is easy to do this accurately if you support the table top on a lump of Blu-tack in a mitre box to keep it level while cutting.) Sand smooth, then reglue the feet with impact adhesive.
4 Paint the table with black satin-finish model enamel.

The low, black 'lacquer' table was inexpensive and heavily varnished. It was cut down from a taller size.

Finding the perfect carpet for a room setting may take time. To make the room look fully furnished while you are searching – or even permanently – try using a paper carpet. Intricately patterned carpets in suitable sizes are often shown in advertisements in decoration magazines and can look surprisingly realistic.

An Art Deco dining room

An Art Deco interior is instantly recognizable. Sinuous furniture with unusual combinations of wood in pale and dark veneers, arranged in segmental patterns, is complemented by the vivid colours of pottery designed by Clarice Cliff, who for many epitomizes this style.

Recently there has been a revival of interest in the unusual furniture and decorative accessories of this period, and as always, professional miniaturists have picked up on this new trend. It is now possible to find 1/24 copies of original furniture and ornaments to complete any room in a typical Art Deco period home.

It is essential to get the background right to set the scene. Pale, painted walls, or boldly patterned wallpapers, and polished wooden floors simulated with 1/24 planking (see page 31) or more simply, in woodgrain paper, are the beginning. Add skirting boards, painted white or cream, and a carpet square; a leather sample, suede side up, will give a feeling of luxury. Charts are available to work a boldly patterned rug or small carpet in Art Deco designs.

A strikingly original Art Deco room, which includes a cocktail cabinet and coffee table, both newly invented items of furniture, and a radio, known as a 'wireless' which would have been made of Bakelite, one of the first plastics. The lampshades are made from Nepalese tissue paper stretched over a brass frame, with rosewood inserts – when wired up the light shines through very effectively. The Clarice Cliff pottery is reproduced in hand-painted porcelain.

Make a fireplace

Like everything else in this newly invented decorative style, fireplaces were original. Buy a simple tiled fireplace, or for economy, make a more unusual version which echoes the curves and ridges on some of the elegant furniture of the time.

You will need:
■ a piece of foamboard or balsa wood approximately ¼in (6mm) thick, 2¾in (70mm) wide by 2½in (64mm) high
■ some finely-corrugated card.

Method

1 Measure and mark the centrepoint and cut out a grate aperture (see page 85). Cut corrugated card to cover the sides and glue on.
2 Cut a piece of the card the width of the fireplace and deep enough to cover the top of the grate aperture, curving it gently up at each side (see picture on page 98). Glue in place.
3 Add a narrow piece of stripwood to form a mantelshelf to hold the essential ornaments.
4 Paint the fireplace with white or cream paint. Glue a piece of black card across the back of the grate aperture.

The hearth

To suit the sophistication of this fireplace design, fit a hearth to simulate polished metal – a piece of not too shiny silver card will be suitable (see picture on page 98). A fan of metal or paper in the grate completes the effect.

A replica of Pierre le Faguays' Archer statuette. The maker's accurately detailed model, cast in pewter, is painted to resemble the original bronze and ivory.

Paint a statuette

Statuettes where the figure is poised for the next movement, such as a dancer or an athlete, were made in bronze and ivory as well as pottery, and needed a high degree of skill from the craftsman.

Cake decorations in the smallest sizes can be adapted as statuettes. Suitable figures can be found but you may have to search to find one small enough. A ballerina will give the idea of movement so important in Art Deco style. Undercoat the figure and then paint to simulate bronze and ivory with model enamel.

The completed statuette of a dancer, painted in bronze and ivory and the 'golfing trophy', painted in silver, are cake decorations. These are too large to suit 1/24 as table decorations, but would look impressive in a hallway or in a large niche.

A 1930s bedroom

Rooms decorated in the early part of this century are period pieces now, but looked ultra-modern in their time. There were jazzy patterns on wallpapers, textiles and carpets, and colour schemes were very different from those we admire today.

Once you find the right backgrounds, it is amazing how quickly your room scheme will fall into place. In the room shown, the pale wood-look paper flooring has a greenish tint which complements the wallpaper, while the

The wallpaper in this room, from a specialist paper supplier, is a bold wavy design which gives the right period impression. The little dog – a dachshund – was a popular breed in the early 1930s, when many wealthy ladies had a small dog as a pet.

floor rug is part of an embroidered silk panel from a greetings card, with an added fringe made from black, stranded embroidery cotton.

Glamour was the key word in the early 1930s, and the period impression can be reinforced by the inclusion of glass ornaments, statuettes and Art Deco pottery (see also page 98).

Furniture

Walnut furniture was admired. Stain simple furniture with walnut woodstain to give the right impression. Make a bed, using a small block of wood or a rigid box – once made up, this economical base will not be seen. The bed

should have a headboard, which again, can be stained, or alternatively painted cream. For the painted version, the edges can be gilded with a gold pen.

Make a headboard

Here are two simple shapes which can be traced and used as a pattern for a headboard to fit a bed 1½in (38mm) wide (3 feet in real size). For a double bed, scale up using graph paper. Cut the headboard from thin wood and stain as walnut; for the painted version use ¼in (6mm) thick card if preferred – once painted, it will look just as good.

The bed is of walnut and the exotic coverlet is made from leopard print ribbon. Use a 1/12 scale ornament if it reinforces a period impression. In the room shown, a Tiffany glass vase adds an extra touch of glamour used as a floor-standing sculpture.

Plain headboard

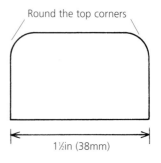

Round the top corners

1½in (38mm)

Create an Art Deco feeling by adding three strips of veneer in an instantly recognizable motif of the time.

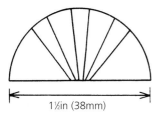

1½in (38mm)

Use a protractor to mark out the angles to fit the veneer strips

Two modern Japanese rooms

It is not difficult to create a modern Japanese room setting which might be recognizable to the young professional in Tokyo or even New York. This is a chance to explore a different environment – the Japanese attitude to interior decoration differs radically from Western ideas.

In Western society, we display our goods for everyone to see. In Japan, valued objects are kept neatly out of sight and brought out only on special occasions, when they can be seen and enjoyed anew.

Both these rooms follow traditional style, but treated in the modern manner now taken up by many younger Japanese. In both rooms, a floor of tatami matting is obligatory, as is a low shelf to display a doll or flower. Colour accents are provided by a lacquer chest, a screen, or a painting on the wall – in real life, not always Japanese, as Western art is now highly regarded.

Tatami matting

To simulate tatami matting, here are two alternative suggestions:

1 **Finely corrugated card**. You will need a natural colour and a darker colour to make the edging, and no painting is necessary.
2 **Wallpaper**. Choose one where the texture will give the impression of woven matting. The reverse side of the paper may be most suitable. Paint it with acrylic paint to achieve the correct colour, using several washes of watered-down paint to vary the shading and give a worn effect.

The mats can be laid out neatly to make a pleasing arrangement. Back with thin card and glue into place. Use a craft knife and raised-edge metal ruler on a cutting mat to make sure that the edges are perfectly straight. Depending on room size, four to six mats will give the right impression in a 1/24 room.

A teapot and two tea bowls are laid out ready for the tea ceremony on a low shelf. The black lacquer writing desk was made in Japan. On the wall, a pictured three-panel screen is used as a painting, and stands out against the black background.

A tea ceremony room

Contrasting textures are important in a mainly monochromatic room where grey, white and black provide elements of light and shade. Try covering one wall with thin black card, another with pale fine voile. Make a low shelf from stripwood approximately ¾in (19mm) deep by ½in (13mm) high. This can be painted black or grey, or fine veneer can be glued on to give a thin wooden surface, as shown.

Small pieces of thin veneer can be found in craft shops or occasionally at craft exhibitions. There are also mail-order stockists who will supply a pack of a selection of Italian, patterned and coloured veneers, for which a miniaturist will find many uses.

The bedroom walls are covered with a white-on-white patterned Japanese paper. A strip of bright orange provides a strong colour accent. A touch of orange is favoured as a contrast to the mainly neutral colours.

Make a 'bamboo' door

To make a door which will let in light and allow a glimpse of a courtyard or garden, try using finely-corrugated card packing from a chocolate or gift box. Cut down alternate grooves of the card to create a slatted effect. Alternatively, a good source of fine bamboo is an inexpensive rattan table mat. Either way, make a door frame from three pieces of thin stripwood.

The Japanese bedroom

A Japanese bedroom is very empty by Western standards. Personal belongings are all stored away in cupboards, which in a full-size room, would have sliding doors and no door furniture.

Make a non-opening cupboard

You will need a piece of balsa wood approximately ½in (13mm) deep, 2in (51mm) wide and the height of the room. Draw a line down the centre. Cut and glue on finely-corrugated card in contrasting colours – one half can be black or dark grey, the other dark blue or light grey. The lines on the card should run vertically on one half and horizontally on the other.

Non-opening cupboard

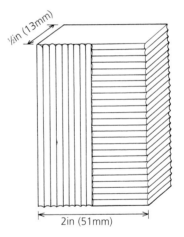

½in (13mm)

2in (51mm)

Make a futon

The futon for the centre of the Japanese room should measure approximately 3in (76mm) long by 1¾in (44mm) wide. For the base, use something fairly stiff, as this should not look soft like a Western mattress. Plasticized card from gift box packing is suitable and can be cut with scissors. Alternatively, use balsa wood.

Cover the base with a scrap of flower-patterned silk and arrange an additional layer of almost transparent paper over it and fold neatly at the corners. (The thinnest dressmaker's interfacing is a good alternative to paper.)

Space is at a premium in modern Japan, where houses are much smaller than in the west. The futon would be stored away during the daytime so that the room could be used for other purposes.

A courtyard

However small the space available, a courtyard of some kind is essential to the modern Japanese home, even if it is arranged in a narrow passageway. The courtyard is not intended to be used, but to be looked at, for contemplation and spiritual refreshment. The fake bamboo doorway in the tea ceremony room (see page 101) gives a tantalizing glimpse of a small courtyard inspired by pictures of modern Japanese garden designs (see Bibliography on page 119).

A small flat wooden box can be used for the courtyard – the sort which contain guest soaps or cigars, are ideal, with sides about 1½in (38mm) high. Stain the sides both inside and out and on top, to make a surround. Line the box with textured paper in grey or stone colour. (Non-clogging finishing paper, a type

of glasspaper with a grey fine-textured finish can be used.)

Choose the objects in the courtyard with care to provide a minimum of detail.

The courtyard measures 6 x 5½ x 1½in (155 x 140 x 38mm) high, and yet contains the essential features of a Japanese garden courtyard. The iris and goldfish are in a tiny pond which measures only ¾in (44mm) in diameter. The pebbles (which came from a Japanese garden in Kyoto) are carefully arranged in groups of three, avoiding the unlucky number four.

Loft living

The huge, wide open spaces of a loft which has been converted to modern living need a no-expense-spared minimalist decor to look good. It would be impossible to fill the rooms with furniture and a few ultra-modern pieces

The modern sculpture was intended for 1/12 scale. Used as a floor-standing piece, it is impressive in the entrance hall to the loft.

emphasize the feeling of space. Cosiness is not, of course, the idea; loft living in London's docklands or in New York's harbour area suits the architect or the film director, who can relax while gazing at wonderful views of waterside and townscape.

A larger size of room box is necessary to reproduce a loft: 12in (330mm) long by 7in (178mm) deep by 7in (178mm) high gives an equivalent ceiling height of 14 feet (4.26m) and the right impression of space. A basic room box of foamboard means that the shiny white surface can be used to represent modern flooring and some of the walls without additional painting or papering.

A room box of this size is large enough to be divided into two spaces. A partition wall of foamboard with a doorway cut out close to the back of the room can be glued in to allow for a hall or a bedroom next to the main room. Create a perspective effect with a suitable picture glued to the back wall of the narrower room, as shown.

Experiment with colour

Yellow and orange are the trendy colours in home furnishings in 1999. Use vividly coloured plain giftwrap on one or two walls to contrast with the white. Add some unframed modern paintings or black and white photographs and, if possible, an impressive piece of sculpture to set the scene. A floor cushion or a large modern sofa (see page 62) and audiovisual equipment made from plastic kits will complete the setting. It is easy to imagine that this is the home of someone working in film or television.

Make a modern table

Use a transparent plastic box as a table, or for an even more unusual effect, cover a small box with metallic card. It is important to colour the edges of the card to avoid white lines showing.

Two vignettes

The dictionary definition of a vignette is 'an ornamental or decorative design of relatively small size'. Although not exact, the miniaturist's term for one of the boxed scenes set in a picture frame is now generally understood.

All the essentials are included in this pretty setting to welcome a new baby. 'Mother' is a lavender bag doll; the stork attached to the wall is a painted cake decoration. The crib and the period perambulator were both professionally made.

Make a vignette box

A ready-made 'picture box' will not be expensive, but if you have a small picture frame you can make one from foamboard. The inside measurements of the frame used for the vignettes shown are 6½in (165mm) wide by 4½in (115mm) high and 2in (51mm) deep, which gives ample room to make a pretty scene.

Measure the frame carefully and cut foamboard to fit into the back of the frame behind the glass. Use the backing card or wood of the frame as a guide to cut the back of the box exactly to size, and glue the sides, top and bottom pieces as shown (see diagram). Line the box with a pretty paper and arrange the scene. It is best to glue tiny objects into place, or fix with double-sided adhesive tape if preferred.

Make a framed box for a vignette

Maximum 2in (51mm) deep

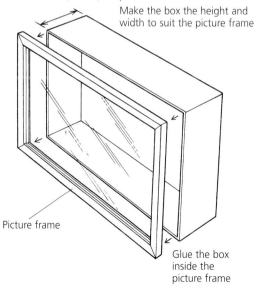

Make the box the height and width to suit the picture frame

Picture frame

Glue the box inside the picture frame

Above Celebrate a child's birthday with plenty of tiny toys.

Push the box firmly into place, adding a dab of glue at the corners. Finally, paper the back and sides of the box to tone with the frame. Hang with picture cord from the hooks on the frame, cutting a long length so that it can be taken across the back of the box and tied firmly before making a loop to hang.

Part Three
Garden & seaside style

A pretty garden with plenty of interest, planned as an addition at the side of a house. A paved path continues behind the house, and the view through the arbour gains an added dimension with a scenic backdrop (cut from a magazine), the edges disguised with added foliage. A mixture of professionally made miniatures and railway model materials works well together.

16 *Making a miniature garden*

Even those who do not enjoy full-scale gardening seem to like creating a miniature garden, either as an addition to their dolls' house or to stand on its own. Creating a garden offers the opportunity to design and make anything you wish, whether it is a replica of your own garden, a period garden to complement the style of you dolls' house, or something more exotic.

Modern garden designers are fond of the concept of a series of garden 'rooms', each one different, and enclosed by hedges or walls. The miniature garden is, in effect, a room, and can be arranged in a two- or three-sided room box. The walls can be clad in brick or stone (see page 110) or provide a base for clipped hedges, trailing plants and foliage.

Before you begin, it is worth browsing through garden books to check out details to suit the chosen period to get the mood right. I have provided plenty of ideas as a starting point for your own variations.

Period gardens

Here are some brief guidelines to achieving the period look in 1/24, and some ideas for modern garden settings too.

Tudor

Tudor gardens were herb or 'knot' gardens. Draw out a design and make neat, geometric beds surrounded by low hedges of box.
- Try using green pan-cleaning pads, trimmed to size, for the hedges.
- Add a dovecote, either free standing or fixed to the house wall.

A dovecote was essential in a Tudor garden, when doves were reared for food. It would make a charming addition to a garden of any period.

Georgian

Georgian gardens too, were very formal. Neat beds, planted with rows of flowers and often with a taller, standard plant in the centre of each bed, were separated by gravel paths. An arbour was provided in which to sit and admire the garden features.

■ To make gravel paths, use textured stencil paint, or cut out from fine sandpaper.

An arbour is one of the smallest of garden buildings, and will make a garden seem inhabited.

Victorian and Edwardian

Victorian and Edwardian gardens relied heavily on bedding plants, and a miniature conservatory or greenhouse would be a great asset (see page 87). Espaliered fruit trees were trained up against brick walls or against the house wall.

■ Metal leaf sprays (see also page 95) in several varieties can be painted and twisted into shape for this purpose. Use tiny wooden or plastic beads, painted as oranges or apples, and fix in place with thin wire threaded through the holes and twisted around the stems.

1930s

A rockery was a feature of the 1930s garden. A small pond was also included if space permitted.

■ Polystyrene packing, crumbled into suitable size pieces, will make lightweight 'rocks'. Paint to resemble stone before fixing into a base of Plasticine moulded into a small mound. There is no need for glue, as Plasticine will fit snugly around the rocks. Provide ground cover with foliage and flowers.

■ Make a pond from fake mirror glass, or by using the method described on pages 51 and 52. Or buy one, made from cast resin – these may also include water plants and goldfish (see page 103).

Modern

The essential feature of a modern garden is a lawn.

■ Simulate with self-adhesive green baize, or railway modeller's grass strip; cut to size and fix in place in one piece.

■ Make paved paths from brick or stone-cladding or use real ceramic flagstones or brick slips (see page 110).

These materials can also be used to construct a complete terrace.

A potting shed will provide useful storage for tools, plant pots or trays of seedlings. This little model can be assembled from a kit.

Garden buildings and follies

Arbours, statues and fountains will enhance your tiny plot, while you can have as much fun decorating a gazebo or summerhouse as a larger project (see also pages 111 and 113).

Above A well makes an interesting feature, especially suited to a cottage garden. This brick-built, slate-roofed example, complete with bucket and chain, can be built from a kit.

Build your own garden feature

A well or modern barbecue corner, depending on the style of your garden, will add interest and also be enjoyable to construct yourself. Kits with straightforward instructions are available to build such a feature in real brick slips to add realism.

17 *Garden settings*

The formal garden

A brick or stone-built gazebo can be the
centrepiece of a small area of formal garden.
In large grounds, a raised, grassy terrace is
usually approached by a path and stone steps,
so that a view of the surrounding garden can
be viewed from the building.

  Surround the setting with tall hedges of
clipped yew (see page 108). Brick cladding
can be glued on to a background wall.

Above left **A gazebo based on a real example at
Hidcote, a beautiful hillside garden in the English
Cotswolds. The maker has reproduced the old
brick in wood, painted in subtle colours. The path
is made from roof tiles.**

Above right **The little gazebo measures only about
3in (76mm) square below the curving roof, but is
large enough to provide useful storage for plant
pots. The walls are lined with thin card depicting
mosaic tiles, which are to scale.**

The English folly

A very grand country house is usually surrounded by parkland extending outside the formal garden, and there will be follies or 'eye-catchers' to impress visitors. In the eighteenth century, Roman temples were popular as follies, and there are still a few remaining to be enjoyed today. The 1/24 Roman temple used as an example here is made of wood, painted with a mix of emulsion and artist's gouache to resemble Cotswold stone.

Alongside this folly, a wooden jigsaw puzzle of a Roman mosaic provides an extension which adds to the effect. This is appropriate, as Roman pavements have been disinterred and preserved in the Cotswolds, the imagined siting of the folly.

Method

1 Apply a base coat of magnolia emulsion.

2 Add a dash of yellow ochre to the emulsion to make a pale yellow. Apply over the base coat and rub off here and there with a damp rag to give a patchy effect.

3 For the second coat, add a little raw sienna to the paint mix, again paint on quickly, rubbing off as you paint to expose some of

the paler shade. To simulate natural weathering, the darker shade should be left under the eaves of the roof and near the base.

4 Finish with a coat of matt varnish.

To fit an imagined placing of this folly in the Cotswolds, the roof is tiled with fibre roofing tiles in a grey-green shade, to represent Cotswold stone. They are cut and distressed by nicking and clipping the edges with tile cutters to simulate weathering. The courses are smaller towards the top of the roof, following local style.

A mosaic floor can be made from museum postcards, cut to fit and glued in place.

A romantic garden

There is nothing more romantic than an old garden with a neglected Gothick folly and plenty of white flowers. This is the sort of garden you sometimes come across in the grounds of an old manor house, a little unkempt but the stuff of fairy-stories.

To achieve the colour of faded eighteenth-century paint which might originally have been a deeper blue or green, first paint with a white base coat of emulsion. Next, paint with two paint mixes, the first in a light and the second in a darker turquoise blue, using the same method as for the Roman folly. A few drops of acrylic or model paint in mid- or deep-blue, stirred into a little pale blue emulsion paint, will make up suitable shades. Finish as before, with a coat of matt varnish.

Brick sheet is again used as a background for this garden, with herringbone bricks laid as a path at the side. The trees and shrubs are railway modelling foliage, which is very suitable for 1/24, while the mossy grass is flock powder in two distinct shades of green, applied over a bumpy base of Plasticine. The path stones are real.

To add to the effect, use a mixture of artificial and real leaves and flowers. Long-lasting gypsophila is a perfect size for the white flowers, and can be supplemented by some fresh rockery flowers in white or mauve, which will need changing regularly.

This little wooden building, with its charming castellations, was copied from an illustration in a magazine. The distressed finish mimics faded original paint.

A Japanese tea garden

To make a Japanese-style garden, you will need to practise painting skills. The greens of the moss are softer than English grass, and although railway modelling materials can be used successfully, it is necessary to tone down the colours with many washes of muted green, brown and grey acrylic paints, well watered down, to achieve the soft effect.

Stones can be made from modelling compound and painted with brown and green diluted acrylic paint. Make trees from fine wire (used to make artificial flowers) twisted together to make the trunk, then the strands twisted out to make first branches and finally

A Japanese tea garden has many things in common with an English garden, but the ground cover is moss, not grass, and has a much softer effect. The trees are distinctive Japanese varieties. The professional maker of this garden also provided the buildings, and the stone lantern, water basin and flume also come from Japan.

twigs. Paint the completed tree with a modelling gel, mixed with paint to add texture.

This is a time-consuming process, and not for the faint hearted, but if you enjoy modelling and admire Japanese gardens, it will be worth all your time and trouble.

Garden ornaments for the Japanese garden

The smallest sizes of pottery buildings sold for use in fish tanks can be adapted to provide a Japanese stone lantern, repainted as stone. Make a water basin from modelling clay, and add a bamboo flume cut from a thin piece of bamboo taken from a rattan table mat. Lash the flume to a bamboo support with strands of raffia.

A Mediterranean courtyard

In hot climates, domestic gardening is often restricted to a courtyard, with shade provided by high walls. This type of inner courtyard provides an oasis of tranquillity in many Mediterranean countries and is used for al fresco lunches and afternoon siestas.

Inspiration for the courtyard shown came from some magazine pictures, which provide the background. The idea of sunshine and shade is crucial to this setting, and the backdrop is arranged to provide one sunny wall while the other is in shade and is painted stone colour. The flagstones are also made of card.

You can almost feel the heat in this sunny courtyard. The setting is complete with a table and a bottle of wine. The pictured flight of stone steps is an effective piece of trompe l'oeil. An orange tree is placed to echo the shadows on the walls, and plants in pots can be moved around.

A Persian garden

A Persian garden brings thoughts of shady spaces, hot sun and turquoise-coloured ceramic tiles. In modern Iran, sunken court-yards surrounded by low walls are still designed to complement modern buildings, with small shrubs in containers which can be moved around to change the scene.

The floor of the courtyard can be repro-duced with card painted with textured paint, in a light sandy colour, by using very fine sandpaper, or as shown, by using handmade paper of a suitable texture and colour. To make a raised edge which can be tiled, use woodstrip and cover it with an Iznik-patterned paper or card – museum postcards of Iznik ceramics will provide many patterns and ideas. Use blue and white miniature ceramic tiles if you feel a little more extravagant – take care

The Persian garden is an imagined setting, turned into a miniature scene. To be successful, it helps to include things which might be present in reality; in this case Iznik tiles seemed essential.

to cut the wood strip to the exact size needed so that the tiles will fit neatly along the top and side edges.

Bronze-patinaed garden ornaments look good in this scheme. To transform metal castings with a verdigris paint finish, first paint with a base coat of pale blue emulsion and follow with a coat of bronze model paint, using the rub-on and rub-off method described earlier (see page 81). Using the same method, add two further coats of paint mix, one of light blue-green and one of a darker blue-green, rubbing off to expose some of the bronze.

A Chinese pavilion

An exotic Chinese pavilion would be an addition to many garden settings. The pagoda in Kew Gardens still delights visitors today, and there are many other examples of oriental-style follies in the gardens of English stately homes – for example at Shugborough Hall, Biddulph Grange, and Stowe, where an eighteenth-century Chinese House has recently been restored and reinstated by the National Trust.

The maker has paid great attention to detail on this tiny pavilion. The gently curving, tiled roof is masterly and the gilded pinnacle and oriental finials add to the exotic style.

18 *Seaside style*

Deckchairs are necessities for a beach scene, and these examples can be folded and taken inside for storage. Choice of materials for such delicate pieces is crucial if they are to fold properly. In this case, canvas is represented by Nepalese tissue paper, striped by hand with a watercolour pencil. The buckets and spades are made of metal recycled from baked bean cans and the design is hand-painted.

scale offers many opportunities to try out skills without taking up too much space or over-spending. I had no idea when I began writing this book that the beach chalet would be one of the projects.

As with so many good ideas, this one came from a glimpse of a miniature building – on this occasion in a dolls' house shop near to the seaside. The original version of the beach chalet was in 1/12, but the maker gladly agreed to make one in 1/24, and this is the result.

Of all the projects I have tackled for this book, the beach chalet with its seaside setting, is among my favourites. It combines

I decided to end this book on 1/24 with a beach chalet in a seaside setting. The dolls' house hobby gives scope for exploring new ideas and developing ways to use them in miniaturized form, and the smaller size of this everything in one tiny space – the fun of mixing paint to achieve just the right colour and degree of weathering, childhood memories, and the joys of a seaside holiday. I hope you enjoy it too.

Shells, sand – and a delicious picnic – the perfect setting for a happy day on the beach.

emulsion paint to give it body). Wipe some of the paint off before it dries, leaving some bare wood showing. Add highlights with a slightly different, brighter shade.

The beach background

- Fine sandpaper simulates a beach. Add some small pebbles and larger stones as 'rocks' to make the background cliffs.
- Use tiny shells brought home from the seaside, or buy packs from gift shops. Add striped blinds or an awning – cut a zigzag edge with pinking shears rather than hemming.
- Make sandcastles from miniature plant pots, turned upside down, with flags of cut paper.
- A party stick 'parasol' can be used as a beach umbrella.
- Provide picnic food – sandwiches and ice-cream wafers. (The food in the setting shown was professionally made.) And for the British beach chalet, at least, cups and saucers for tea are essential.

Decoration

First choose the colour scheme. This is one dolls' house project where you can use bright colours to advantage. Blue, green, purple or yellow are all colours traditionally used for beach huts to make a rainbow effect on holiday resort beaches. Add some white for contrast.

The weathered look

Alternatively, you might decide to go for a weathered, slightly shabby look. This is achieved by sponging on a thin acrylic paint mix (add a little water and a small amount of

Bibliography

Battersby Martin, *The Decorative Twenties*, revised edition, The Herbert Press 1988

Battersby Martin, *The Decorative Thirties*, revised edition, Whitney Library of Design N.Y. 1988

Brunskill, Ronald and **Clifton-Taylor**, Alec, *English Brickwork*, Ward Lock 1977

Christy Geraldine and **Pearch** Sara, *Step-by-Step Art School Ceramics*, Chartwell Books Inc. 1991

Clifton Taylor, Alec and **Ireson**, A.S., *English Stone Building*, Victor Gollancz 1983 (new edition, reprint 1994)

Innes, Jocasta, *Scandinavian Painted Decor*, Cassell 1990

Jones, Anthony, *Charles Rennie Mackintosh*, Studio Editions 1990

Jones, Barbara, *Follies and Grottoes*, Constable 1973

Lyall, Sutherland, *Dream Cottages*, Robert Hale 1988

MacQuoid, Percy, *A History of English Furniture*, reprint Bracken Books 1988

Miller, Judith, *Period Fireplaces*, Mitchell Beazley 1995

Oster, Maggie, *Japanese Garden Style*, Quarto 1993

Parissien, Steven, *The Georgian Group Book of the Georgian House*, Aurum Press 1995

Pfeiffer, Walter (Photographs) and **Shaffrey**, Maura (Text), *Irish Cottages*, Weidenfeld and Nicolson 1990

Prizeman, John, *Your House the Outside View*, Quiller Press 1982

Quiney, Anthony, *The Traditional Buildings of England*, Thames and Hudson 1990

Slesin, Suzanne, **Cliff**, Stafford and **Rozensztroch**, Daniel, *Japanese Style*, Thames and Hudson 1987

Snodin, Michael and **Stavenow-Hidemark**, Elisabet (Editors), *Carl and Karin Larsson, Creators of the Swedish Style*, V & A Publications 1997

Van de Lemme, Arie, *A Guide to Art Deco Style*, Quintet Publishing 1987

Walker, Aidan, *Wood Polishing and Finishing Techniques*, Swallow Publishing 1985

Walshe, Paul (Text) and Miller, John (Pictures), *French Farmhouses and Cottages*, Weidenfeld and Nicolson 1992

Makers of featured dolls' houses & miniatures

Jill Bennett, dolls p.43

David Booth, Chippendale chairs p.8 and p.86, double-ended sofa p.40 and p.78

Borcraft Miniatures, wall-hanging shelves p.10 and p.61, Victorian kitchen p.15, Grannie's cottage interior p.69, wood mouldings pp. 71–82, 1930s lounge p.92

Clive Brooker, plant pots p.60 and p.61, 'stone' bench and planter p.107, plant pots used as sandcastles p.117 and p.118

Brooklea Crafts, Tudor 'hutch' p.79, Tudor chair p.80, chest p.80 and p.81, garden rose arbour and trellis p.107

Michael Browning, polished wooden dolls' house p.32, polished wooden shop p.91

Lesley Burgess (Miniature Dreams), teatime food p.90 and p.118

Neil Carter, modern sculpture, p.16 and p.103, Art Deco figure p.99

Wendy Chalkley (Dolls of Distinction), Regency dolls p.44, Charles II doll p.45

Malcolm Chandler, 1/24 chest of drawers p.7, dresser p.69

Dave Chatterton ('Les Chats'), painted houses and shop p.32

Chicken Little Miniatures, baby's crib p.104, Lloyd Loom chair p.42 and p.118

Christopher Cole, child's dolls' house p.2

Jeremy Collins (Gable End Designs), early Victorian house p.87, porch/window p.24, Aga p.61 and p.82

Country Harvest, bread p.61, beehive p.107

Glenda Cunningham, cottage p.18, doorway p.23, interior p.56, cottage interior p.68

Matthew Damper, Art Deco furniture p.42 and p.98

John Davenport, Dutch bureau cabinet p.5

Jacqui Dennison (Frontshop Miniatures), TV from plastic kit p.60 and p.103, stereo (kits) p.103, garden shed from kit p.109

Frances England (England's Magic), Victorian house p.19

John Finn, corner cupboard p.79

Phillip Freemantle, oak refectory table p.41 and p.82

Bryan Frost, millhouses p.14, p.49, p.50, p.51, p.53 and p.60, Yeoman's house (part decorated) p.51

Greenleaf, dolls' house made from kit p.13

James Hemsley (Trigger Pond Dolls' Houses), Wealden House p.49, Tudor house interior p.52

The Heritage Doll Company, doll from kit p.45

Honeychurch Toys Ltd, Georgian dolls' houses p.1, p.19, p.25, p.34 and pp.71–82

Tony Hooper, fireplaces with grates (cast resin) p.80

Muriel Hopwood, 1/24 porcelain bowl p.7

Houseworks, Shenandoah Furniture, rocking chair, p.40, doughbox p.61

David Hurley, carved oak chests p.7, carved Tudor bed p.58

Jackson's Miniatures, shops from plans, p.91

Japanalia, traditional room box p.20, Japanese tea garden p.113

Tony Knott, armour, weapons, pewter tableware p.57

Laurence and Angela St. Leger, carousel and clown p.105, buckets and spades p.117 and p.118

Lilydale Designs, dovecote p.108

Coleen and Valentine Lyons, Tudor dolls p.45

Peter Mattinson, medieval/Tudor house p.18, medieval door and window p.22

Merry Gourmet Miniatures, flowers p.90 and p.95, bonsai p.101

Miltonduff Miniatures, modern piano and stool p.43, spinet p.78

Mouse House Miniatures, salami p.82, fruit in bowls p.79 and p.82

Pam Paget-Tomlinson, embroidered bed hangings p.58

G. J. Parker, inter-war house p.21, doorway/window p.24

Peppermint Designs, 1930s-style carpet kit/chart p.90, Art Deco-style carpet kit/chart p.98

Pat Pinnell, house made from plans by Derek Rowbottom, p.48

Colin and Yvonne Roberson, metal chairs p.7, p.80 and p.100, 'marble'-topped table p.82 and p.114, 1930s gas stove p.90, Victorian perambulator p.104

Rosedale, fireplaces (cast resin) p.78 and p.79, range (kitchen picture) p.89

Rowen Dolls' Houses, house with electric lighting, p.38

Brian and Eileen Rumble (Rudeigin Beag), Scottish 'but and ben' p.65, interior of 'but and ben' p.68

Harry Saunders (Daydream Dwelling), cottage with electric lighting p.38, Tudor window p.23, cottage p.66

Chris Sheppard (Shepwood Dolls' Houses), beach chalet p.117 and p.118

Margaret Sitch, knitted lace bed hangings p.7 and p.80

Carol Slater, 'tapestry' p.56

Richard Stacey, cladding (on mill made by Bryan Frost) p.49, brick and slate p.84, well made from kit p.110

Stillmore Homes, cottage ornée p.13, black-and-white timbered house p.50, arbour p.109, Chinese garden pavilion p.116

Tetbury Miniatures, prie-dieu chairs p.8 and p.41

Penny Thomson, medieval/Jacobean dolls' house p.13, 'dancer' doll in papier-mâché p.44, house with 'stone' cladding p.51, thatched cottage p.64

Keith Thorne, cottages p.15, American Colonial house p.17, Fishermen's cottages p.19, Regency house p.33, Georgian table p.41, cottage ornée p.66, toll house p.67, cottage interior p.68, gazebo p.111, Gothick folly p.113

Jenny Till, Auricula in pot p.61, small pond with iris and fish p.103, box with lettuce and snail p.107

Toptoise, Mackintosh-style dolls' houses p.20, Edwardian doll's house p.21, shop/cafe p.22, door/window p.24, Mackintosh interior p.39, Mackintosh-style longcase clock p.42, row of shops p.90, Victorian villa p.88, Mackintosh room box setting p.93

Mr Uchiyama, Japanese thatch p.67

Pat Venning, Art Deco porcelain p.42 and p.98

Warwick Miniatures, pewter saucers p.10 and p.61, pewter coffee pot p.61, cups and saucers p.118

Trevor Webster, interior of Wealden house under construction p.49

June and Albert Wells, cottage p.65, cottage with garden p.70, bird bath with flowers p.107

Paul Wells, cottage p.12, Hall of Mirrors p.39, Georgian town house p.83, doorway/window p.23, medieval/Tudor Guildhall p.47, brick cladding in sheet form p.83, p.111 and p.113

Geoffrey Wonnacott, chess table and set p.6

World of My Own, house interior p.54

Yesteryear Homes, Tudor houses p.6

Metric conversion table

Inches to millimetres and centimetres

mm – millimetres   cm – centimetres

inches	mm	cm	inches	cm	inches	cm
⅛	3	0.3	9	22.9	30	76.2
¼	6	0.6	10	25.4	31	78.7
⅜	10	1.0	11	27.9	32	81.3
½	13	1.3	12	30.5	33	83.8
⅝	16	1.6	13	33.0	34	86.4
¾	19	1.9	14	35.6	35	88.9
⅞	22	2.2	15	38.1	36	91.4
1	25	2.5	16	40.6	37	94.0
1¼	32	3.2	17	43.2	38	96.5
1½	38	3.8	18	45.7	39	99.1
1¾	44	4.4	19	48.3	40	101.6
2	51	5.1	20	50.8	41	104.1
2½	64	6.4	21	53.3	42	106.7
3	76	7.6	22	55.9	43	109.2
3½	89	8.9	23	58.4	44	111.8
4	102	10.2	24	61.0	45	114.3
4½	114	11.4	25	63.5	46	116.8
5	127	12.7	26	66.0	47	119.4
6	152	15.2	27	68.6	48	121.9
7	178	17.8	28	71.1	49	124.5
8	203	20.3	29	73.7	50	127.0

About the author

Jean Nisbett began to take notice of period houses, their decoration and furniture before she was ten years old, and they have been a consuming passion ever since. While bringing up a family she turned this interest to the miniature scale, and restored, decorated and furnished many dolls' houses. Her houses have been shown on Channel 4, BBC Television and TFI France.

She began writing while working in the London offices of an American advertising agency, and is well known as the leading British writer in the dolls' house field. Her articles have appeared regularly in specialist miniatures and dolls' house magazines since 1985, as well as in home decoration magazines. This is her fourth book for GMC Publications. She lives in Bath.

Index

TITLES AVAILABLE FROM
GMC PUBLICATIONS
BOOKS

Dolls' Houses & Miniatures

Architecture for Dolls' Houses	*Joyce Percival*
Beginners' Guide to the Dolls' House Hobby	*Jean Nisbett*
The Complete Dolls' House Book	*Jean Nisbett*
The Dolls' House 1/24 Scale: A Complete Introduction	*Jean Nisbett*
Dolls' House Accessories, Fixtures and Fittings	*Andrea Barham*
Dolls' House Bathrooms: Lots of Little Loos	*Patricia King*
Dolls' House Fireplaces and Stoves	*Patricia King*
Easy to Make Dolls' House Accessories	*Andrea Barham*
Heraldic Miniature Knights	*Peter Greenhill*
Make Your Own Dolls' House Furniture	*Maurice Harper*
Making Dolls' House Furniture	*Patricia King*
Making Georgian Dolls' Houses	*Derek Rowbottom*
Making Miniature Gardens	*Freida Gray*
Making Miniature Oriental Rugs & Carpets	*Meik & Ian McNaughton*
Making Period Dolls' House Accessories	*Andrea Barham*
Making Period Dolls' House Furniture	*Derek & Sheila Rowbottom*
Making Tudor Dolls' Houses	*Derek Rowbottom*
Making Unusual Miniatures	*Graham Spalding*
Making Victorian Dolls' House Furniture	*Patricia King*
Miniature Bobbin Lace	*Roz Snowden*
Miniature Embroidery for the Georgian Dolls' House	*Pamela Warner*
Miniature Embroidery for the Victorian Dolls' House	*Pamela Warner*
Miniature Needlepoint Carpets	*Janet Granger*
The Secrets of the Dolls' House Makers	*Jean Nisbett*

Toymaking

Designing & Making Wooden Toys	*Terry Kelly*
Fun to Make Wooden Toys & Games	*Jeff & Jennie Loader*
Making Board, Peg & Dice Games	*Jeff & Jennie Loader*
Making Wooden Toys & Games	*Jeff & Jennie Loader*
Restoring Rocking Horses	*Clive Green & Anthony Dew*
Scrollsaw Toys for all Ages	*Ivor Carlyle*
Scrollsaw Toy Projects	*Ivor Carlyle*
Wooden Toy Projects	*GMC Publications*

Woodworking

40 More Woodworking Plans & Projects	*GMC Publications*
Bird Boxes and Feeders for the Garden	*Dave Mackenzie*
Complete Woodfinishing	*Ian Hosker*
David Charlesworth's Furniture-making Techniques	*David Charlesworth*
Electric Woodwork	*Jeremy Broun*
Furniture & Cabinetmaking Projects	*GMC Publications*
Furniture Projects	*Rod Wales*
Furniture Restoration (Practical Crafts)	*Kevin Jan Bonner*
Furniture Restoration and Repair for Beginners	*Kevin Jan Bonner*
Furniture Restoration Workshop	*Kevin Jan Bonner*
Green Woodwork	*Mike Abbott*
Making & Modifying Woodworking Tools	*Jim Kingshott*
Making Chairs and Tables	*GMC Publications*
Making Fine Furniture	*Tom Darby*
Making Little Boxes from Wood	*John Bennett*
Making Shaker Furniture	*Barry Jackson*
Making Woodwork Aids and Devices	*Robert Wearing*
Minidrill: 15 Projects	*John Everett*
Pine Furniture Projects for the Home	*Dave Mackenzie*
Routing for Beginners	*Anthony Bailey*
Router Magic: Jigs, Fixtures and Tricks to Unleash your Router's Full Potential	*Bill Hylton*
Router Projects for the Home	*GMC Publications*
The Scrollsaw: Twenty Projects	*John Everett*
Sharpening Pocket Reference Book	*Jim Kingshott*
Sharpening: The Complete Guide	*Jim Kingshott*
Space-Saving Furniture Projects	*Dave Mackenzie*
Stickmaking: A Complete Course	*Andrew Jones & Clive George*
Stickmaking Handbook	*Andrew Jones & Clive George*
Test Reports: *The Router* and *Furniture & Cabinetmaking*	*GMC Publications*
Veneering: A Complete Course	*Ian Hosker*
Woodfinishing Handbook (Practical Crafts)	*Ian Hosker*
Woodworking Plans and Projects	*GMC Publications*
Woodworking with the Router: Professional Router Techniques any Woodworker can Use	*Bill Hylton & Fred Matlack*
The Workshop	*Jim Kingshott*

Woodturning

Adventures in Woodturning	*David Springett*
Bert Marsh: Woodturner	*Bert Marsh*
Bill Jones' Notes from the Turning Shop	*Bill Jones*
Bill Jones' Further Notes from the Turning Shop	*Bill Jones*
Bowl Turning Masterclass	*Tony Boase*
Colouring Techniques for Woodturners	*Jan Sanders*
The Craftsman Woodturner	*Peter Child*
Decorative Techniques for Woodturners	*Hilary Bowen*
Essential Tips for Woodturners	*GMC Publications*
Faceplate Turning	*GMC Publications*
Fun at the Lathe	*R.C. Bell*
Further Useful Tips for Woodturners	*GMC Publications*
Illustrated Woodturning Techniques	*John Hunnex*
Intermediate Woodturning Projects	*GMC Publications*
Keith Rowley's Woodturning Projects	*Keith Rowley*
Make Money from Woodturning	*Ann & Bob Phillips*
Multi-Centre Woodturning	*Ray Hopper*
Pleasure and Profit from Woodturning	*Reg Sherwin*
Practical Tips for Turners & Carvers	*GMC Publications*
Practical Tips for Woodturners	*GMC Publications*
Spindle Turning	*GMC Publications*
Turning Miniatures in Wood	*John Sainsbury*
Turning Wooden Toys	*Terry Lawrence*
Turning Pens & Pencils	*Kip Christensen & Rex Burningham*
Understanding Woodturning	*Ann & Bob Phillips*
Useful Techniques for Woodturners	*GMC Publications*
Useful Woodturning Projects	*GMC Publications*
Woodturning: Bowls, Platters, Hollow Forms, Vases, Vessels, Bottles, Flasks, Tankards, Plates	*GMC Publications*
Woodturning: A Foundation Course (New Edition)	*Keith Rowley*
Woodturning: A Fresh Approach	*Robert Chapman*
Woodturning: A Source Book of Shapes	*John Hunnex*
Woodturning Jewellery	*Hilary Bowen*
Woodturning Masterclass	*Tony Boase*
Woodturning Techniques	*GMC Publications*
Woodturning Tools & Equipment Test Reports	*GMC Publications*
Woodturning Wizardry	*David Springett*

WOODCARVING

The Art of the Woodcarver	*GMC Publications*	Understanding Woodcarving	*GMC Publications*
Carving Birds & Beasts	*GMC Publications*	Understanding Woodcarving in the Round	*GMC Publications*
Carving on Turning	*Chris Pye*	Useful Techniques for Woodcarvers	*GMC Publications*
Carving Realistic Birds	*David Tippey*	Wildfowl Carving - Volume 1	*Jim Pearce*
Decorative Woodcarving	*Jeremy Williams*	Wildfowl Carving - Volume 2	*Jim Pearce*
Essential Tips for Woodcarvers	*GMC Publications*	The Woodcarvers	*GMC Publications*
Essential Woodcarving Techniques	*Dick Onians*	Woodcarving: A Complete Course	*Ron Butterfield*
Lettercarving in Wood: A Practical Course	*Chris Pye*	Woodcarving: A Foundation Course	*Zoë Gertner*
Power Tools for Woodcarving	*David Tippey*	Woodcarving for Beginners	*GMC Publications*
Practical Tips for Turners & Carvers	*GMC Publications*	*Woodcarving* Tools & Equipment Test Reports	*GMC Publications*
Relief Carving in Wood: A Practical Introduction	*Chris Pye*	Woodcarving Tools, Materials & Equipment	*Chris Pye*

UPHOLSTERY

Seat Weaving (Practical Crafts)	*Ricky Holdstock*	Upholstery Restoration	*David James*
Upholsterer's Pocket Reference Book	*David James*	Upholstery Techniques & Projects	*David James*
Upholstery: A Complete Course (Revised Edition)	*David James*		

CRAFTS

American Patchwork Designs in Needlepoint	*Melanie Tacon*	An Introduction to Crewel Embroidery	*Mave Glenny*
A Beginners' Guide to Rubber Stamping	*Brenda Hunt*	Making Character Bears	*Valerie Tyler*
Celtic Cross-Stitch Designs	*Carol Phillipson*	Making Greetings Cards for Beginners	*Pat Sutherland*
Celtic Knotwork Designs	*Sheila Sturrock*	Making Hand-Sewn Boxes: Techniques and Projects	*Jackie Woolsey*
Celtic Knotwork Handbook	*Sheila Sturrock*	Making Knitwear Fit	*Pat Ashforth & Steve Plummer*
Collage from Seeds, Leaves and Flowers	*Joan Carver*	Natural Ideas for Christmas	*Josie Cameron-Ashcroft & Carol Cox*
Complete Pyrography	*Stephen Poole*	Needlepoint: A Foundation Course	*Sandra Hardy*
Contemporary Smocking	*Dorothea Hall*	Pyrography Designs	*Norma Gregory*
Creating Knitwear Designs	*Pat Ashforth & Steve Plummer*	Pyrography Handbook (Practical Crafts)	*Stephen Poole*
Creative Doughcraft	*Patricia Hughes*	Ribbons and Roses	*Lee Lockheed*
Creative Embroidery Techniques Using Colour Through Gold	*Daphne J. Ashby & Jackie Woolsey*	Rubber Stamping with other Crafts	*Lynne Garner*
		Tassel Making for Beginners	*Enid Taylor*
Cross Stitch Kitchen Projects	*Janet Granger*	Tatting Collage	*Lindsay Rogers*
Cross Stitch on Colour	*Sheena Rogers*	Temari: A Traditional Japanese Embroidery Technique	*Margaret Ludlow*
Decorative Beaded Purses	*Enid Taylor*	Theatre Models in Paper and Card	*Robert Burgess*
Designing and Making Cards	*Glennis Gilruth*	The Creative Quilter: Techniques & Projects	*Pauline Brown*
Embroidery Tips & Hints	*Harold Hayes*	Wool Embroidery & Design	*Lee Lockheed*
Glass Painting	*Emma Sedman*		

THE HOME & GARDENING

Home Ownership: Buying and Maintaining	*Nicholas Snelling*	Security for the Householder: Fitting Locks and Other Devices	*E. Phillips*
The Living Tropical Greenhouse	*John and Maureen Tampion*	The Birdwatcher's Garden	*Hazel and Pamela Johnson*

VIDEOS

Drop-in and Pinstuffed Seats	*David James*	Twists and Advanced Turning	*Dennis White*
Stuffover Upholstery	*David James*	Sharpening the Professional Way	*Jim Kingshott*
Elliptical Turning	*David Springett*	Sharpening Turning & Carving Tools	*Jim Kingshott*
Woodturning Wizardry	*David Springett*	Bowl Turning	*John Jordan*
Turning Between Centres: The Basics	*Dennis White*	Hollow Turning	*John Jordan*
Turning Bowls	*Dennis White*	Woodturning: A Foundation Course	*Keith Rowley*
Boxes, Goblets and Screw Threads	*Dennis White*	Carving a Figure: The Female Form	*Ray Gonzalez*
Novelties and Projects	*Dennis White*	The Router: A Beginner's Guide	*Alan Goodsell*
Classic Profiles	*Dennis White*	The Scroll Saw: A Beginner's Guide	*John Burke*

MAGAZINES

Woodturning • Woodcarving • Furniture & Cabinetmaking • The Dolls' House Magazine
The Router • The ScrollSaw • Creative Crafts for the Home • BusinessMatters • Water Gardening

---

The above represents a full list of all titles currently published or scheduled to be published.
All are available direct from the Publishers or through bookshops, newsagents and specialist retailers.
To place an order, or to obtain a complete catalogue, contact:

GMC Publications

Castle Place, 166 High Street, Lewes, East Sussex BN7 1XU, United Kingdom Tel: 01273 488005 Fax: 01273 478606

Orders by credit card are accepted